Connecting Brain Research with Effective Teaching

The Brain-Targeted Teaching Model

Mariale M. Hardiman

A SCARECROWEDUCATION BOOK

The Scarecrow Press, Inc.
Lanham, Maryland, and Oxford
2003

A SCARECROWEDUCATION BOOK

Published in the United States of America
by Scarecrow Press, Inc.
A Member of the Rowman & Littlefield Publishing Group
4501 Forbes Boulevard, Suite 200, Lanham, Maryland 20706
www.scarecrowpress.com

PO Box 317
Oxford
OX2 9RU, UK

British Library Cataloguing in Publication Information Available

Library of Congress Cataloging-in-Publication Data

Hardiman, Mariale M. (Mariale Melanson), 1951–
   Connecting Brain Research with Effective Teaching : the Brain-Targeted
Teaching Model / Mariale M. Hardiman.
      p. cm.
   "A ScarecrowEducation book."
   Includes bibliographical references and index.
   ISBN 0-8108-4632-2 (Paperback : alk. paper)
  1. Educational psychology. 2. Learning—Physiological aspects.
3. Brain. 4. Teaching—United States—Psychological aspects. 5. School
improvement programs—United States. I. Title.
LB1057 .H27 2003
370.15—dc21

2002015988

This book is dedicated to my husband and children, Bob, Tara, and Krysta, whose unending love, support, and encouragement led me through every page.

It is also dedicated to my parents, Gloria and Paul, and to my brothers and sisters: Michelle, Tony, Paula, Greg, Vince, and Matt.

Finally, it is written in loving memory of my brother John Melanson.

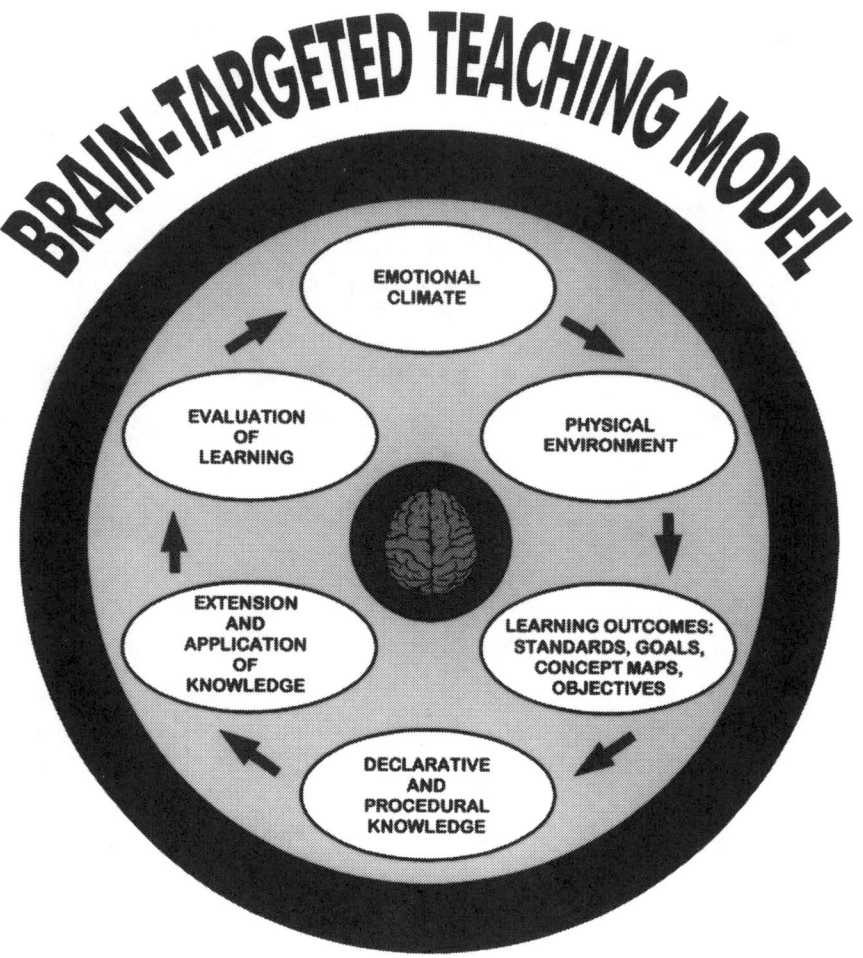

Contents

Acknowledgments

This book could not have been written without the continual support and advice of my friend and colleague, Gordon Porterfield. From conception to completion, he freely gave of his time and expertise to read, reread, edit, suggest, and encourage. His spirit is embedded in these pages as much as my own.

I am indebted to Dr. Steven Hsiao, neuroscientist at the Mind/Brain Institute of The Johns Hopkins University, for his expert advice, suggestions, and encouragement. I would also like to thank the many teachers who contributed to this work by submitting lesson plans, offering ideas, and providing research: Michelle Hartye, Paula Mainolfi, Elayne Melanson, Robin Melanson, Gwyn Powell, Marty Sharrow, Kathy Rivetti, Catherine Gearhart, Kelly Reitschel, Linda Bluth, Susan Rome, Laurie Frank, Gordon Porterfield, Claire Grizzard, Joan Schenkel, Karl Sanzenbacher, Dan Hellerbach, Kristine Jost, Teresa Stroebel, Deb Ptak, Kay Hellwig, Bill Ruffin, Dot Sell, Carolyn Freeland, Maxine Brooks, Brenda Abrams, and Sam Clayton.

I would like to acknowledge Dave Mattheiss for creating the brain-targeted teaching model graphic, Bennett Grizzard for his drawings of the brain in chapter 1, Lamonica Mountain for designing the learning unit template, and Johns Hopkins professor Dr. Peggy King-Sears for her advice on the article I wrote for the November 2001 issue of *Educational Leadership*, "Connecting Brain Research with Dimensions of Learning," which is how this book began.

Introduction

Teachers have seen educational reforms come and go. Ask a group of veteran teachers how many of the new educational initiatives they have fully incorporated into their teaching, and an honest response will often be a wink and a smile. The truth is that, despite mountains of reform initiatives, little actual change has occurred in American classrooms during the last several decades.

Take Ms. Gordon, for example. She has taught sixth grade in a suburban school district for the past 19 years. She works hard to try to implement all the educational reforms promoted by her school district. Yet this experienced teacher feels inadequate:

> Every time I turn around, a new program is presented that will "reform education." If you wait long enough, that program will fade and a new one will take its place. Just when I had my classroom set up for mastery learning, for example, cooperative learning became the vogue. The next focus was teaching to students' learning styles, followed by teaching higher-order thinking skills. Then we were presented with discovery-learning, performance-based assessment, and portfolio assessment, in rapid succession. Now, after last year's emphasis on differentiating curriculum and instruction, we're being trained in collaborative learning communities. We have also been exhorted to integrate into our curriculum a host of topics such as technology education, arts education, character education, violence prevention, service learning, drug education, and so forth. Now this "integrated curriculum" must align with new state standards so that our students will perform well on state tests. Although my students perform above national norms, I still feel enormous pressure

to continually improve scores on our state's accountability testing. At the same time, I want to foster a joy for learning so that my students' classroom experience becomes more than simply test preparation.

Ms. Gordon's experience is not unique. Many teachers feel overwhelmed by the plethora of educational reforms and the pressure to raise test scores. It's no surprise that beginning teachers typically feel this burden to an even greater extent. Let's look at Mr. Johns' experience as a first-year teacher of social studies. He believed that his fifth-grade students had mastered the objectives of the curriculum, yet their performance on the end-of-year assessment proved that they had retained little of the content and skills he thought he had taught during the school year. Mr. Johns wondered how his teacher preparation program could have better prepared him for the complexities of teaching in today's classrooms. He wished he had acquired a better understanding of those teaching strategies that would have made his content more exciting for his students and would have resulted in meaningful, lasting learning.

My experience leading schools and instructing graduate students has convinced me that most teachers, like those described above, *want* to implement the best of what research and practice tell us is effective instruction. Yet they are constantly bombarded by new initiatives without being given a system to help them integrate these initiatives into classroom practice.

My own quest for education's magic bullet led me in the mid-1980s to study brain research, which focused mainly on left/right brain studies and included the seminal work of neuroscientists such as Dr. Marian Diamond and Dr. Michael Gazzaniga. These studies in the 1980s preceded an explosion of brain research that has opened up new horizons about how we think and learn. I wondered at first if this attention to brain research was merely another fad or if it could truly help educators discover the best methods for teaching children. My own studies have since convinced me that brain research supports much of what experience and research tell us is effective instruction. Most important, studying brain research has helped me to determine which instructional strategies foster true learning. Yet, despite so much current attention, the findings of brain research are still not readily accessible to classroom teachers. I believe that teachers, as well as administrators and policy-makers, need a framework that integrates these findings into a coherent system connecting brain research with components of effective teaching.

This book is designed to do just that. It will present a model of instruction that targets what we now know supports how the brain thinks and learns. This instructional framework, which I've called the brain-targeted teaching model, does not purport to be a new method of teaching. Rather, it provides a format for using current brain research to guide teachers in planning, implementing, and assessing a sound program of instruction. It is my hope that the model will increase the potential of brain research not only to inform instructional strategies but also to suggest ways to organize schools and curricula to enhance teaching and learning. Its focus, however, is on classroom instruction, which is where authentic educational reform must take place. Its primary audience, then, is educational practitioners and those who guide and support them. As a practicing principal of a large, urban K–8 school and as a graduate education instructor, I interact with a wide range of teachers in both public and private schools throughout the state of Maryland and beyond. Their contributions to this book have been essential, giving the work its authenticity.

The book is divided into three parts. Chapters 1 through 3 provide a description of brain anatomy, a synthesis of important findings of current brain research, and an introduction to the brain-targeted teaching model as a system for enhancing student learning. Chapters 4 through 9 describe the components of the brain-targeted teaching model, analyzing each one in terms of its connections to the findings of brain research. These chapters include practical applications of each component of the model as they follow Mr. Johns, the first-year teacher described above, through the planning and implementation of his first unit of instruction for the new school year. Finally, chapters 10 and 11 provide field-tested learning units based on the brain-targeted teaching model and sample school improvement plans that school administrators could use to create schools that support brain-based learning.

A final observation: The reauthorization of the Elementary and Secondary Education Act (ESEA) requiring annual standards-based testing in grades 3–8 has aroused heated debate in the educational community.

Many educators fear that an emphasis on high-stakes accountability testing will cause schools and teachers to focus their priorities on test preparation rather than on developing the wide range of learning activities that brain research supports. Although it would not be wise for educators to shrink from accountability, I firmly believe that we must view high performance on standardized assessments of basic skills not as the goal of instruction, but only as a beginning—a launching point, as it were, to true learning that must, as brain research insists, emerge from experience.

CHAPTER 1

The ABCs of Brain Anatomy

Teachers are educators, not neurobiologists. . . . Do we really need to know brain structure and function to be effective teachers? The truth is, no; you could quickly skip to chapter 3 and implement brain-targeted teaching methods without knowing how the brain actually works. A fundamental understanding of the structures and functions of brain, however, will allow us, as educators, to comprehend the workings of the incredible brain and become better consumers of the mountains of research that have emerged since the 1990s, which was designated by the scientific community as the "decade of the brain." Perhaps this new decade and new century should be dubbed "the decade of teaching to the brain" to recognize the need to design practical applications of neuroscience to the teaching and learning process.

AMAZING BRAIN FACTS

Weighing in at about three pounds, the brain has the size of a grapefruit and the shape of a nut. It is made up of about 78% water, 10% fat, and 8% protein. The brain's one hundred billion (100,000,000,000) cells use about eight gallons of blood per hour and need about eight glasses of water per day. Although the brain makes up less than 2.5% of the body's total weight, it consumes about 20% of the body's energy—10 times the rate of the rest of the body. This enormous energy consumption is needed to process an amazing amount of information, estimated to be between 10 to the

27th power and 10 to the 100 billionth power bits of data per second (Greenleaf, 1999).

BRAIN ANATOMY

The human brain is composed of identifiable structures, the organization of which we will examine first from back to front, then from left to right.

The Hindbrain

The hindbrain contains the *brain stem*, which includes the *medulla oblongata*, the *pons*, and the *cerebellum* (see Figure 1.1). Scientists believe that the brain stem is the oldest part of the evolving brain, controlling such autonomic functions as breathing, heartbeat, blood circulation, tongue movements, and vocal sounds. Sensations such as touch, taste, and sound pass through the medulla oblongata in the brain stem before moving to the cerebral cortex for conscious awareness. The pons controls facial expressions and chewing and connects the brain stem to the cerebral cortex (Diamond & Hopson, 1998). Within the brain stem is a system of neurons known as *reticular formation* (RF), which regulate all vital life-support systems of the body as well as involuntary movements such as pupil constriction. Another vital function of the RF is the *reticular activating system* (RAS), which controls the body's sleep and arousal systems. The RAS also controls how information is received in the brain by filtering sensory information and allowing us to focus on a stimulus and ignore background information. Your students' RAS is hard at work if they are focusing on your voice and ignoring the hum of fluorescent lights overhead or the distant sounds of traffic on the street.

At the back of the skull, attached to the brain stem, is the cerebellum, which controls the body's execution and planning of movement and balance. The cerebellum serves as a conductor of the body's muscle systems, directing muscle groups to work together to produce harmonious movements needed to perform the simplest or most complex motor activities. When a certain movement is repeated over and over, the

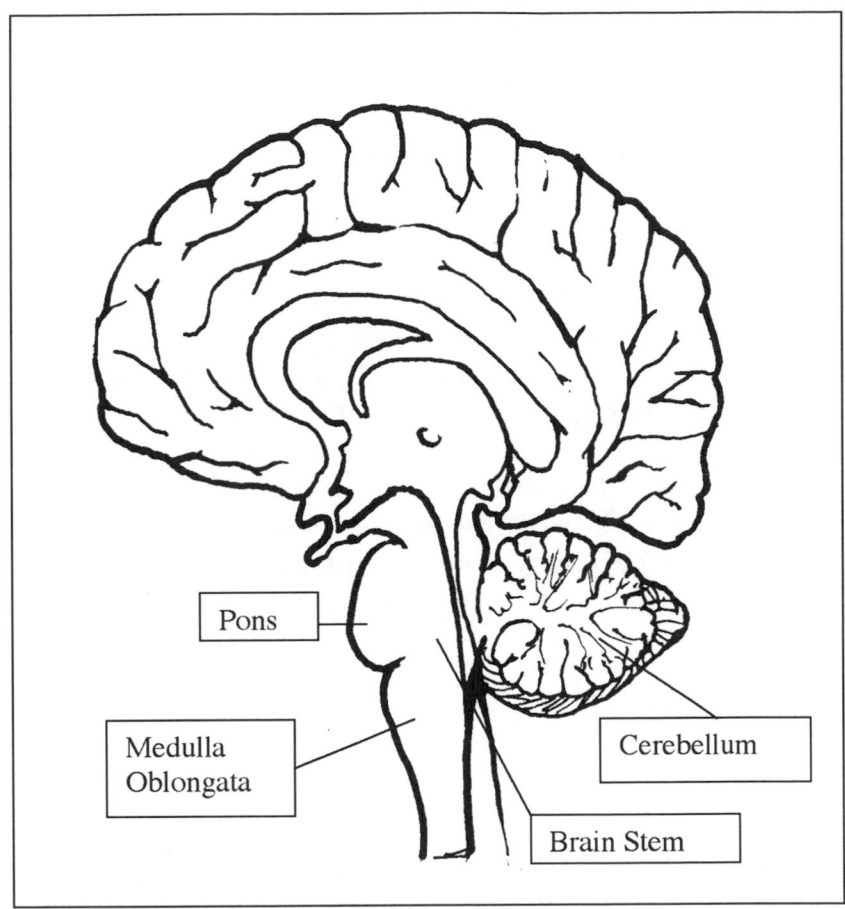

Pons

Medulla
Oblongata

Cerebellum

Brain Stem

Figure 1.1. *The hindbrain.*

cerebellum stores it so that it becomes automatic, not needing conscious thought to perform the skill. When children first learn to write their names in cursive, for example, they must concentrate on how to form each stroke. When these movements are stored in the cerebellum's kinesthetic memory, this skill becomes fluid and automatic. The cerebellum is hard at work storing repeated motor memories, from hitting that perfect serve in tennis, to riding a bike, to signing hall passes. Recently, scientists have come to believe that the cerebellum stores not only automatic motor activity but also repetitive learning, such as the alphabet, multiplication tables, and the blending of phonemes into words (Sprenger, 1999).

The Limbic System

Located just above the brain stem is the limbic system, known to control our emotions. This system connects the lower parts of the brain responsible for automatic and motor functions with the higher cerebral cortex, the area responsible for cognitive thought. The parts of the limbic system that most influence learning are the *thalamus, hypothalamus, hippocampus,* and *amygdala* (see Figure 1.2).

Thalamus. In our brain's core is the thalamus, a walnut-sized structure that directs information between our senses and our cerebral cortex. After receiving information, the thalamus relays it from all senses except smell to other parts of the brain for further processing.

Hypothalamus. Just as the thalamus relays external information to various parts of the brain, the hypothalamus relays internal information to certain areas of the brain. The hypothalamus controls the process of homeostasis, regulating and adjusting the body's functions to maintain a normal state. For example, the hypothalamus increases perspiration

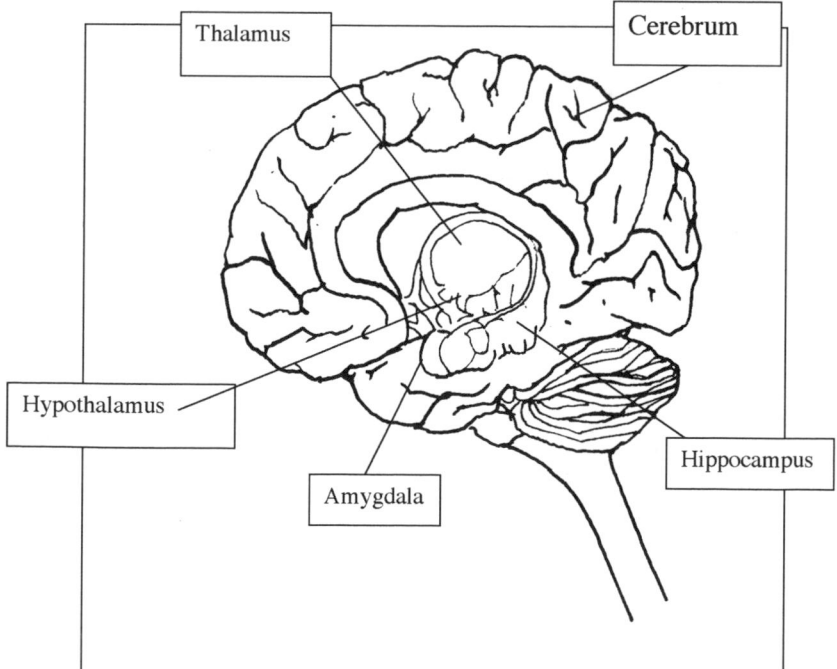

Figure 1.2.   The cerebrum and limbic system.

to lower body temperature when it bec⋯ regulates appetite and induces the body's fig⋯ it senses danger, adjusting in a split second the⋯ up to increase heart rate and respiration.

Hippocampus. Shaped like a seahorse, the hip⋯ workhorse of the brain's memory system. It holds⋯ the immediate past and compares it to experiences stored⋯ memory, a process essential for creating meaning. Once e⋯ stored in the hippocampus, some will eventually become long⋯ memory, moving from storage in the hippocampus to the co⋯ (LeDoux, 1996).

Amygdala. The amygdala is an almond-shaped structure most often cited as playing a central role in the control of emotions. This structure receives information from the thalamus and evaluates it relative to its emotional content. If the amygdala senses threat or danger, it sends a signal to the hypothalamus, which relays the message to the endocrine system to increase hormones to raise heart rate and blood pressure and ready our muscles for activity. Scientists believe that the emotional component of an experience is stored in the amygdala, while more factual events related to the experience, such as where or when the event occurred, are stored in other parts of the brain. According to LeDoux (1996), the amygdala receives a stimulus 40 milliseconds before the intellectual centers of the brain. When you see a log that looks like a snake, for example, you may initially experience a fear response because the brain's logical center has not yet processed the fact that the object is only a log and not a snake.

The Cerebrum

The largest and most complex section of the brain, the *cerebrum*, is divided into two sections, referred to as cerebral hemispheres (see Figure 1.2). The left and right hemispheres of the cerebrum are connected by a thick bundle of nerve fibers called the *corpus callosum,* which allows the two sides of the brain to function as one unit. Each hemisphere controls motor activity on the opposite side of the body. Covering the cerebrum is a 1/10th-inch layer of tissue rich in nerve cells and connecting fibers called the *cortex*. Its surface area appears as

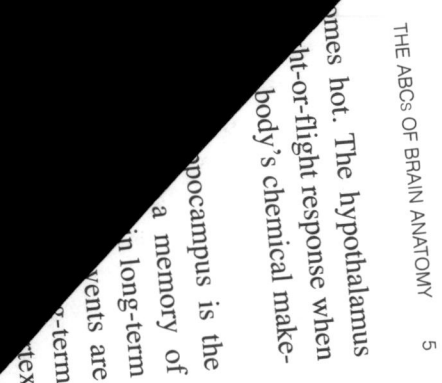

mes hot. The hypothalamus
ht-or-flight response when
body's chemical make-

pocampus is the
a memory of
n long-term
ents are
-term
tex

: about the size of a large
up 80% of the total brain
a million miles of nerve
each controlling a differ-

rests the occipital lobe,
visual stimuli. As visual
it to the visual cortex to
previously stored mem-

e located in the left and
hey are responsible for
recognition, such as object shapes, in addition to processing auditory stimuli. The left hemisphere temporal lobe contains
Wernicke's area, the seat of our understanding of spoken language.

Parietal lobe. Located on the top and along the sides of the head,
each parietal lobe receives sensory information from the opposite side

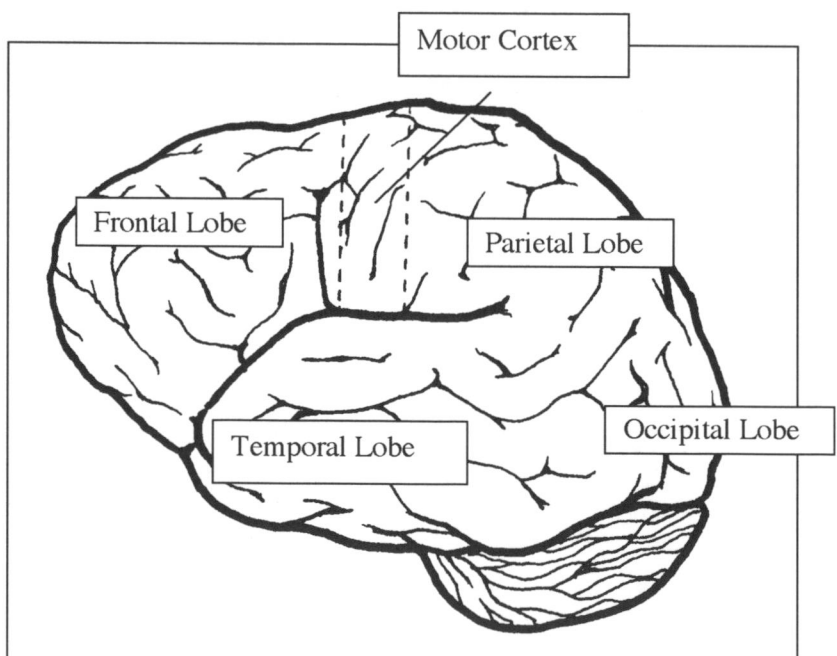

Figure 1.3. *The four lobes and motor cortex.*

of the body. The parietal lobes include the sensory strip, which receives and processes stimuli of pain, pressure on the skin, body position, temperature, and touch. It is also responsible for locating where things are in the world relative to our bodies, allowing us to grasp objects, and redirecting our focus of attention to new salient stimuli in the environment.

Frontal lobe. The front of the cerebrum holds the brain's thinking center, the area responsible for working memory, higher-order thought, problem-solving, and language. The frontal lobe contains our speech center, known as Broca's area. At the back of the frontal lobe, just in front of the parietal cortex, are a set of cortical areas involved in movement. They allow for decision-making, motor planning, and motor execution.

Left Brain/Right Brain

Studies of hemispheric specialization that emerged during the 1970s and 1980s sparked much popular interest in our "two-sided brain." We learned that the left hemisphere is largely the language center of the brain and engages in logical, sequential information processing. Scientists believe that the left hemisphere is analytical and attends to detail, while the right hemisphere may be responsible for generalized concepts. Researchers believe that the right hemisphere processes sensory stimuli and thinks in pictures rather than words. It manages information in a holistic fashion; our intuitive and creative thinking is centered in this hemisphere.

The concept of cerebral dominance emerged from left/right brain studies and led us to believe that an individual's style of thinking and behaving reflected the influence of one hemisphere over another. Scientists maintained that artists, for example, who displayed superior visual-spatial skills, had a dominant right hemisphere, whereas people who excelled at manipulating language, like lawyers, were thought to have a dominant left hemisphere.

We now know that this distinction is rather simplistic. Although recent research has confirmed the specialization of our brain hemispheres, we also know that the two hemisphere are continuously working in tandem to produce the rich complexities of human thought.

Listening to our favorite song, for example, involves both the right hemisphere, as we enjoy the sounds of harmony and rhythm, and the left hemisphere, as we analyze the song's components, instruments, and words.

Brain Cells

So far, we have examined the structures of the brain. Now we will focus on brain cells and the fascinating process of cell communication—the essence of learning. The brain's 100 billion cells are made up of two basic types, *neurons* and *glial* cells.

Neurons. Comprising one-10th of the brain's cells, neurons look like bulbs with sprouting roots and a long tail (see Figure 1.4). The "roots" are called *dendrites* and function as antennae that receive information from other neurons, distant or nearby, or from the brain's environment (Diamond & Hopson, 1998). The "tail," called the *axon,* performs the task of carrying messages away from nerve cells to the dendrites of other cells, which then transmit the information to their cell bodies. The process is repeated when the receiving cell sends the signal through its axon to yet another cell, which, in turn, receives the signal through its dendrites. During this process, axons and dendrites never actually touch. The electrical impulse that flows from the axon travels over a small gap called a *synapse* through chemicals, *neurotransmitters,* that are stored in sacs, called *synaptic vesicles*, located at the end of each axon (see Figure 1.5). Frequently used axons send information faster. These axons are surrounded by *myelin*, a fatty sheath that forms around axons to speed up the electrical transmission and reduce interference from other cell activity. These electrical impulses are known to travel at speeds of up to 220 miles per hour (Greenfield, 1997).

As we can see, the axon sends information through both electrical and chemical signals. The brain's chemicals, neurotransmitters such as endorphins, dopamine, serotonin, serve to either excite or inhibit cell activity.

Glial cells. Glial cells make up about 90% of the brain. Their function is to support neural activity by producing myelin to coat the neural axons, transporting nutrients and waste to and from the brain, as well as protecting neurons from harmful substances.

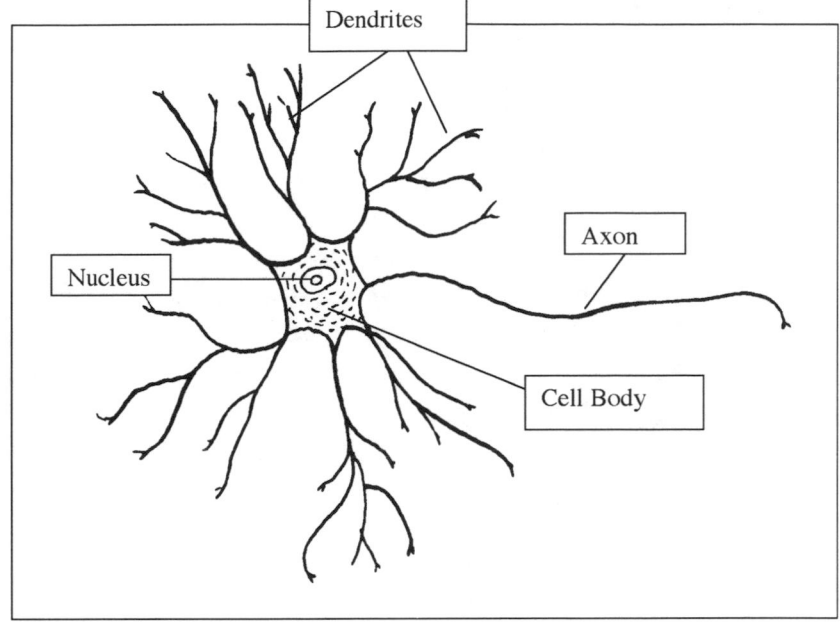

Figure 1.4. *Neurons.*

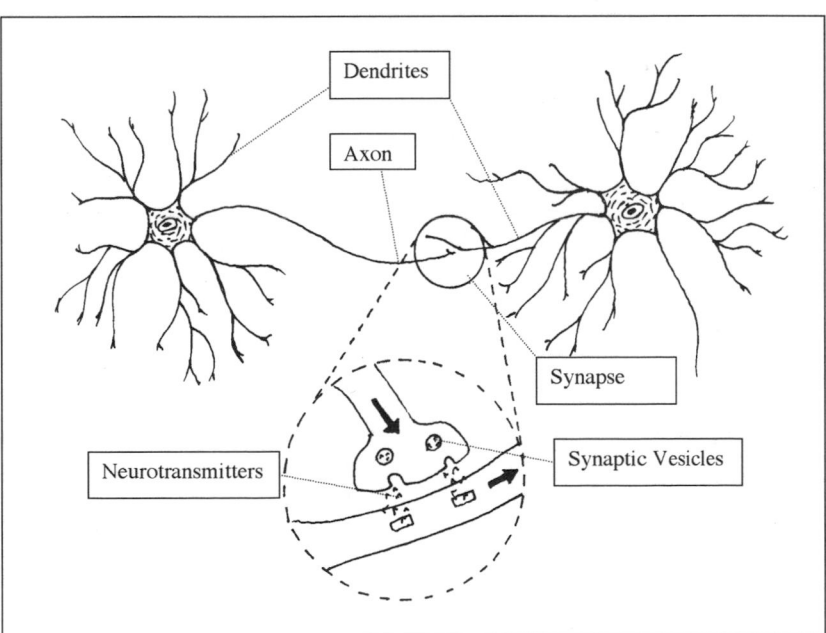

Figure 1.5. *Cell communication.*

HOW THE BRAIN LEARNS

As you may know, the human brain has all its cells from birth. (Only recently have researchers discovered that the hippocampus appears to generate new cells in adults as a result of physical activity.) If we don't grow new brain cells, then how do we learn? Learning is about connections. Surprised? We shouldn't be. As educators, we see every day that the process of teaching and learning requires a connection between teacher and learner. This connective process, although interpersonal, is also neurobiological. When axons send signals that are received by dendrites, learning takes place. The more such connections are made, the faster and more efficiently the signals move, thereby facilitating learning. New learning creates new pathways, causing the growth of more dendrites. You thought you were only teaching algebra? You were also facilitating the growth of dendrites. If the brain perceives that quadrilateral equations are worth retaining, this information is committed to areas of the brain that store long-term memories, a process called long-term potentiation (LTP).

In chapter 2, we will explore LTP and other concepts, such as *plasticity*, *sensitive periods,* and *neurobiological differences,* to understand how they inform teaching and learning and how they relate to our brain-targeted teaching model.

Important Themes in Brain Research

Now that you have become excited (I hope) about how the brain works, we should review some of the general principles that have emerged from brain research during the past two decades. Much of this research was made possible because of advances in brain imaging techniques, which have allowed scientists to test the brains of people who are still alive and well. In the early days of brain research, this was not possible. In 1861, for example, Paul Broca discovered that the frontal lobe of the left hemisphere (now called Broca's area) was responsible for speech production. His discovery was based on the study of a man who had lost total speech following a stroke. Broca wisely waited until the man's death to perform the autopsy that led to this discovery. Advanced imaging techniques performed on the patient's brain (found years later in a Paris museum) demonstrate that Broca was right. Luckily, scientists can now learn about the complexities of the human brain by using state-of-the-art technology to study live subjects.

BRAIN IMAGING TECHNIQUES

X Rays

Most of us are familiar with X rays used to determine if bones are broken. When a bone is X-rayed, radiation from electromagnetic waves is partially absorbed into the bone. The rest of the radiation strikes a photographic plate, leaving an imprint of the bone. The shadings of the

X ray depend on the degree of denseness of the object. A bone appears white, while soft tissues are dark. Until the 1970s the X ray was the only technique available for imaging the structure of a living brain. But the X ray has little application for brain research, because the brain is composed of soft tissue.

Computerized Axial Tomography (CAT) Scans

The use of CAT scans was a major advance over the X ray in learning about brain structure. Because the CAT scan gathers information from many positions around the patient's head, a three-dimensional image can be calculated. It also generates slices of various planes through the brain, allowing neurologists to view internal structures. CAT scans are useful to detect tumors or brain lesions.

Electroencephalograpy (EEG)

The EEG measures brain-wave frequency, the electrical patterns caused by neural activity. Scientists measure a patient's brain waves by placing on the patient's scalp sensors connected to the EEG, which then records the patient's brain signals on a monitor or chart. The EEG, commonly used during the 1980s in left/right brain studies, is still useful for detecting episodes of epilepsy or determining a subject's state of arousal.

Positron Emission Tomography (PET) Scans

PET scans allow researchers to view areas of the brain that are working while a person performs a particular activity. Radioactive glucose is injected into the subject, who is then placed in a PET scanner and asked to perform mental tasks. Computerized images are created to demonstrate areas of the brain that produce the highest levels of glucose while the subject performs each task. PET scans allow scientists to view an active brain at work. Its colored images are frequently included in journals that contain studies of brain research. Red, yellow, and white areas indicate high activity; blue, green, and purple show areas of lower brain activity.

Magnetic Resonance Imaging (MRI)

MRI technology uses a strong magnetic field and the body's own resonating water molecules to give off radio signals that are assembled into a computer image. The MRI can provide information about the flow of blood to regions of the brain and about the metabolic state of selected brain regions. The MRI produces clearer images than the CAT scan and can show the internal brain structures from any angle.

Functional Magnetic Resonance Imaging (fMRI)

The fMRI uses MRI technology to track brain activity while a subject is engaged in a mental task. As blood flows to the areas of the brain where the activity is processed, oxygen in the blood changes the magnetic field so that radio signals become more intense. A computer image is produced during the performance of the activity.

IMPORTANT THEMES IN BRAIN RESEARCH

Although brain research is generally conducted by medical practitioners who specialize in neurology, its findings have enormous implications for educators. Several general themes, which have emerged during the last 20 years of brain research, are discussed below.

Plasticity

When children in your classrooms learn, their brains change in structure and chemistry. This concept is called plasticity. Neuroscientist Marian Diamond, from the University of California at Berkeley, conducted research in the 1980s that investigated changes in the structure of nerve cells in the cerebral cortex of rats when they were exposed to two different environments. Diamond placed one group of rats in an enriched environment that included a wide variety of objects, such as exercise wheels, platforms, and ladders; another group was placed in an impoverished environment, consisting only of a cage without toys. The rats in the enriched environment showed greater facility in running different kinds of mazes than did the rats in the impoverished environment. Most remarkable, however, is that the rats living in the enriched environment developed a thicker cerebral cortex, while those living in the impoverished environment showed a thinning of the cortex (Diamond & Hopson, 1998).

Diamond's study demonstrates that the cortex grows through experiences. As we know from chapter 1, new experiences stimulate nerve cells, causing them to grow dendrites, which form connections to other cells. Each of our 100 billion brain cells receives input from as many as 20,000 other nerve cells. Just think of the connections that occur every minute when the brain is stimulated! The best news for those of us concerned with middle-aged memory loss is that these same brain changes were found in young and middle-aged rats, as well as in rats that were the equivalent of 90-year-old humans. We now know that the brain changes at any age; the "use it or lose it" adage is clearly at work for both rats and humans, whether 9 months or 90 years old!

Sensitive Periods

Another common theme that has emerged from brain research is the concept of "windows of opportunity," those sensitive periods in a child's development when optimal learning is best achieved. The notion of windows of opportunity for learning was first reported in the early 1800s in the classic work of a French doctor, Gaspard Itard. This work, *The Wild Boy of Aveyron*, describes Itard's attempts to educate a preadolescent mute boy found in the wild forests of Aveyron where, having apparently been abandoned, he survived by living with animals. It was assumed that, because the child had no human role models for language, he had not acquired speech. Itard took the child to live with him and designed multiple methods to educate Victor, as he called him. Although the boy learned to perform many tasks, he never learned to speak. Victor's window of opportunity for speech had passed, leading researchers to wonder for years afterward what mechanisms were no longer available to Victor's brain.

Neurologists now know that about 200 billion neurons are formed in the first four months of the growing embryo's life, but that about half will die off during the fifth month. While this natural pruning process occurs, the brain is growing dendrites. While the number of cells is diminishing, the connections among them are increasing exponentially — at a rate of up to 3 billion a second. From birth to age 10, the connections among brain cells rise rapidly, then slowly decline throughout the remainder of a person's life.

Diamond and Hopson (1998) explain that, because of this neural sculpting, childhood is a critical time for brain development. Connections among well-used brain cells are strengthened, while unused cells are weakened and pruned. This natural pruning is essential for the human brain to focus—to be able to use certain circuits for performing tasks necessary to the developing child's brain. We know that before age 10 damage to parts of a child's brain may be less traumatic because of the brain's ability to adjust and transfer the function of the damaged part of brain to healthy parts. In adults, however, recovery from trauma is usually slower and less complete.

Researchers have found that certain windows of opportunity close completely if the brain does not receive environmental stimulation. Other windows remain open, but learning occurs less easily. For example, vision is a function that requires early stimuli for normal development. If the child's brain does not receive visual stimuli by age 2, the person will be forever blind (Sousa, 2001). Researchers at Johns Hopkins and Harvard universities performed experiments in the 1960s that demonstrated the importance of visual stimuli. They sewed shut the left or right eye of a kitten for several months, then opened it and studied the cat's eye and visual cortex. They found that, if the eye was closed from day 30 to day 80, the cat was blind in that eye. Children also have a critical period for vision, as well as for hearing and language development. Such a critical period for hearing, for example, appears to take place four to five weeks after conception. If a mother contracts certain viral infections during this time, the child may be born deaf or hearing-impaired. Language also appears to have a critical period. If a child does not hear human language (as in the case of the boy from Aveyron), the neural pathways that would normally activate language learning are lost by about age 10.

Wolff and Brandt (1998) point out, however, that not all windows of opportunity close as tightly as those for vision, hearing, and language. Although with some difficulty, adults can learn a second language; however, if the phonology of the language is not heard in early life, the adult learner will likely speak with an accent. Adults can learn other activities, such as riding a bike or playing a musical instrument, but the learning will be slower and more laborious. Although childhood is an important time for learning, we know now that the brain possesses a limitless capacity to reorganize itself to acquire new learning at any age.

Learning and Memory

Cognitive scientists have identified multiple memory systems in the brain, each devoted to different memory functions.

Short-term memory. Short-term memory allows us to retain information (e.g., a phone number for immediate use) for the time such information is needed, then discard it. David Sousa (2001) explains that short-term memory generally holds data for about 30 seconds, depending on its importance to the individual.

Working memory. Working memory, like short-term memory, is a temporary storage system, but it also allows us to perform executive functions such as planning, organizing, and rehearsing (Wolff, 2001). The brain is able to chunk information, whether letters, numbers, or ideas, in the working memory system to a capacity of about seven items (LeDoux, 1996). LeDoux explains that we use working memory in our current thinking to embody the information, ideas, and thoughts that we are currently attending to and processing. The capacity of our working memory increases with age. It is active for preadolescents for about 5 to 10 minutes, for adolescents and adults for 10 to 20 minutes, after which times the average person loses focus (Sousa, 2001).

Long-term memory. Working memory also draws from the information stored in long-term memory. Marilee Sprenger (1999) identifies five types of memories stored in long-term memory: semantic, episodic, procedural, automatic, and emotional. She explains that these memories are retrieved through "memory lanes" in the brain. Semantic memory holds information learned from words; episodic memory relates to space and location. Both semantic and episodic memories are processed through the hippocampus. Procedural memory, processed through the cerebellum, is the memory of muscle activities, such as riding a bike or hitting a baseball. Automatic memory, also processed in the cerebellum, stores information (e.g., letter sounds, number values) so we can automatically recite the alphabet, decode words, or retain multiplication facts. Emotional memory is processed through the amygdala, which, as we know, filters the emotional content of all information received by the brain. If information is "emotionally charged," the amygdala sends out hormones such as cortisol to ready the body's system for stress. We will examine the connections between emotions and learning in chapter 4.

Long-term potentiation (LTP) and long-term depression (LTD). LTP and LTD represent the latest research by neuroscientists into how the brain stores information at the cellular level. LTP refers to the strengthening of synaptic connections between neurons after the neurons have received stimulation, and LTD refers to the weakening of synaptic connections. In a recent study at Brown University, Memgia-Seraina Rioult-Pedotti and her team of researchers taught rats to reach into a hole in a box to grasp food pellets. After five days, the researchers found that, in addition to retaining the new skill, the rats' brains had changed. The strength of the synaptic connections between neurons in the motor cortex had increased (Turner, 2000). Clearly, neurobiological changes are at work when the brain learns new information.

Neurobiological Differences in Students with Learning Disabilities and Attention Deficits

While neurobiological research is shedding light on how the brain learns, researchers are also discovering fundamental differences in how children with attention deficit and learning disabilities process information. Margaret Semrud-Clikeman and her colleagues (2000) used MRI scans to study students who were diagnosed with attention deficit and hyperactivity disorder (ADHD). She found that, compared to control groups without ADHD, children with ADHD demonstrated neuroanatomical differences that compromised the alerting and executive networks of the brain. She also found that differences in the frontal lobe of the right hemisphere resulted in compromised automaticity and reduced speed of response to stimuli.

Neurobiologists are also learning more about brain differences in children with learning disabilities. For more than 50 years, neurologists and educators suspected that learning disabilities had neurological origins, but now scientists have produced evidence that such disabilities are indeed biologically based. Shaywitz et al. (2001) conducted multiple studies that confirm a "biological signature for reading disability" (p. 245). Their 1998 study, for example, used the fMRI to measure the flow of blood to sections of the brain responsible for language while subjects performed tasks requiring phonological processing. They found significant differences in brain functioning between students with reading disabilities and nonimpaired readers. As the level of difficulty of the phonological tasks increased, students with reading disabilities failed to increase activation in brain regions responsible for language. The researchers concluded that the underactivation of posterior brain regions, those responsible for language, and the overactivation in anterior regions provide a neural marker for reading disabilities.

Differences in brain scans of poorly performing readers also occur regardless of which language students speak. Researchers used PET scans to observe differences in neural activity in the temporal lobe, the language center, of disabled and nondisabled readers while reading texts in English, French, and Italian. In all three languages tested, the researchers found that subjects with reading disabilities showed less neural activity in the language centers of the brain than did nonimpaired readers (Helmuth, 2001). The researchers assert that students with reading disabilities have fewer neural connections among cells in the language regions of the brain.

Richards and his team of researchers at the University of Washington found neurochemical differences in the brains of reading-disabled adolescent boys when compared to matched nonimpaired readers (Richards et al., 2000). While subjects performed tasks requiring language processing, the researchers measured and mapped the production of lactate in areas of the brain that produce language sounds. Compared to good readers, boys with reading disabilities showed four times as much lactic acid production. Lactic acid is a by-product of the metabolism of glucose and an indicator of exertion by brain cells. This study shows that poor readers work harder than good readers to perform the same language tasks. Richards and his colleagues administered to the students with reading disabilities an intensive, three-week, phonics-based instructional intervention and enriched science instruction. Results of follow-up tests revealed both significantly improved reading skills and a decline in the production of lactic acid for students with reading disabilities. Thus, intensive instruction resulted in greater efficiency of brain functions and greater proficiency in reading.

BRAIN-TARGETED TEACHING

In this chapter, we have explored how the brain is sculpted by our experiences. We know that, although the potential for brain growth is limitless through old age, the optimal time for learning some important human functions, such as language, occurs in the early years of a child's life. Research also tells us that effective instruction not only increases memory and learning but also produces neurobiological changes in the brain. What better reason to implement a model of teaching that draws from research-based effective instruction and is tied to what we know about how the brain thinks and learns? In the next chapter we will look at the brain-targeted teaching model and explore additional themes in brain research, such as modular brain components and the limbic system, to see how they relate to the components of brain-targeted teaching.

CHAPTER 3

The Brain-Targeted Teaching Model

Mr. Johns, now beginning his second year of teaching, approaches the new school year with excitement and trepidation. He hopes to convey his love of history to his fifth-grade students; yet he wants his students not only to demonstrate mastery of the content but also to be able to apply concepts and skills beyond the classroom to real-life problem-solving. Along with beginning-of-the-year jitters, Mr. Johns is tackling fundamental questions about the very nature of teaching and learning:

- What content, skills, and processes must his students know? How will he select learning goals and objectives? How will he make these goals meaningful to students?
- What will he do to help his students acquire this knowledge? How will he accommodate the individual needs and learning styles of his students?
- What activities will help his students review and practice this knowledge so that they can retrieve it when needed?
- How will he help his students integrate this knowledge with what they already know and apply it to future learning?
- How will his students apply this knowledge meaningfully in real-world settings?
- How will he know that his students have learned?

After his experiences as a first-year teacher, Mr. Johns knows that his teaching techniques must change. He realizes now that his students were frequently bored by the material and assignments he gave them.

He knows that his methods, which relied heavily on lectures, discussion, and independent student work, must expand to include more active learning experiences. Having heard how the results of brain research can be applied to learning, Mr. Johns hopes to adopt teaching strategies that parallel what neuroscience tells us about the nature of learning. He looks to the brain-targeted teaching model to provide him with guidelines and strategies as he embarks upon a new school year that he hopes will result in challenging yet meaningful learning experiences for his students.

This model does not propose new methods of teaching. Rather, it synthesizes a number of elements related to research-based effective teaching and connects each one to what neuroscience reveals about how the brain learns. This model is intended to help teachers who feel overwhelmed as they attempt to integrate recent educational reforms into instructional practice. Folded into the brain-targeted teaching model are the major features of effective instruction. I hope that, if the suggestions in this book are followed, the teaching and learning process will prove to be fulfilling for both students and teachers.

BRAIN-TARGETED TEACHING MODEL

The brain-targeted teaching model describes six stages of the teaching and learning process. Although each stage is explored as a separate component, the stages are interrelated. That is, the principles applied in the first stage, setting a positive emotional climate for learning, apply throughout all other stages of the model. Evaluating instruction, the last stage, infuses the entire process of brain-targeted teaching. The components of the model include:

Brain Target 1 (BT-1): Setting the Emotional Climate for Learning

Chapter 4 explores the important connection of emotions and learning. Setting the emotional climate in the classroom is an essential part of a teacher's instructional program. Brain research supports the notion that a positive emotional climate paves the way for higher levels of learning and performance. On the other hand, a threatening, stressful learning environment can significantly impede learning. This chapter explores the effect of self-concept on learning, examines structures and functions in the brain's emotional center, and identifies factors that cause stress for students in school. It suggests strategies for reducing stress and promoting a positive emotional environment in the classroom.

Brain Target 2 (BT-2): Creating the Physical Learning Environment

The classroom environment can be a powerful tool for focusing students' attention and offering them a secure and supportive learning experience. Chapter 5 examines how novelty in the classroom, through the regular adjustment of classroom displays and seating, can foster attention. It also explores how lighting, sound, and scents can influence the learner. Strategies are recommended to provide optimal learning environments.

Brain Target 3 (BT-3): Designing the Learning Experience

In chapter 6 we explore what neuroscientists tell us about the brain's search for meaning and relevancy amidst the continuous sensory input that it processes. We will look at how the brain uses prior knowledge to categorize stimuli into concepts that are either familiar or novel and then combines these concepts to create new patterns of thinking and understanding. BT-3 promotes the use of concept maps to give students "big picture" ideas or global understanding of concepts, as well as to connect these ideas to their prior knowledge and understanding. Additionally, this chapter demonstrates how content standards can be used to create learning goals and outcome-based instructional objectives that describe what students will know and do as a result of instruction.

Brain Target 4 (BT-4): Teaching for Declarative and Procedural Knowledge

In chapter 7, we explore learning and memory. We will view how an experience is encoded, processed, stored, and retrieved in short-term, working, and long-term memory systems. BT-4 then demonstrates the best instructional practices to target what we know about the processes used by the brain to acquire and store information.

Brain Target 5 (BT-5): Teaching for Extension and Application of Knowledge

Expanding on BT-4, chapter 8 discusses the concept of the modular brain, exploring how the use of active learning experiences engages multiple brain systems. BT-5 recommends the use of instructional strategies that extend and refine students' learning, encouraging the meaningful use of acquired knowledge in active, real-world problem-solving tasks.

Brain Target 6 (BT-6): Evaluating Learning

Evaluating instruction is as important to the learning process as meaningful learning activities. In chapter 9 we examine how evaluation in this model expands the traditional types of assessments to include the use of oral and written probes, rubrics, student portfolios, student-generated products, and performance-based assessments.

Let us now consider how emotions color everything that we think, feel, and learn as we explore brain target 1 in the next chapter.

CHAPTER 4

Brain Target 1 (BT-1)
Setting the Emotional Climate for Learning

The first component of the brain-targeted teaching model focuses on the vital role that emotions play in learning. Like most teachers, Mr. Johns knows intuitively that the attitudes of his students affect their learning. During the school year, he watched the learning process shut down when a student experienced a crisis in his or her life; he observed how the delight of a humorous moment could light up a lesson; he noticed that students were suddenly attentive when discussing an event that triggered strong emotions; he agonized over the poor performance of students whose anger seemed to impede learning. Indeed, within a few months of teaching, Mr. Johns understood that it is impossible to separate emotions from learning. Brain research now supports what he suspected: Educators can promote academic success for students by reducing stressful classroom environments and by using positive emotional experiences to enhance learning.

In the brain-targeted model, setting the emotional climate in the classroom may be the most important function that teachers perform each day. A positive emotional climate paves the way for higher levels of learning and performance. This chapter will explore the effect of self-concept on learning, examine structures and functions in the brain's emotional center, identify factors that cause stress for students in school, and suggest strategies for reducing stress and promoting a positive emotional environment in the classroom.

CASE STUDY: BREAKING THE CYCLE OF FAILURE

For many of our students, optimizing learning may require simple adjustments in classroom routines or the inclusion of strategies to enhance the connections of emotions to learning. Some students, however, have been disenfranchised from our schools and classrooms. Reconnecting these students to a meaningful and supportive school experience may require more drastic measures to break the cycle of failure that comes from low expectations, insecurity, and poor self-esteem. One such case follows.

In the early 1980s, Sharon taught remedial reading in an urban middle school in Baltimore with a large population of children from economically disadvantaged homes. Her students had poor reading performance; all had histories of school failure. Their classroom behaviors demonstrated lack of motivation and frustration with school. Many were regularly truant from school or from her class.

After several years of struggling with unmotivated students, Sharon was desperate for strategies to reconnect her students to school success. She decided to try a technique that she had experienced at a local university in a summer program designed to help adults overcome math phobia. During the course, the students worked out a set of problems every Thursday; on Friday, these same problems were given to the class on a quiz. Sharon, along with most of the other students in the class, passed every quiz with flying colors. Gradually, different problems were placed on the Friday quiz until, by the end of the course, Sharon was successfully completing a variety of problems that she had never seen before. She was pleased with her success and proud that she had overcome her math phobia.

Hoping such a technique would work with her own students, Sharon taught a "practice quiz" to her class on Thursday of every week. On the following day, the students received the same items on a real quiz. As most students did well on the Friday quizzes, their grades for her class began to rise. Better grades, however, were not the only outcome of this new strategy. To Sharon's surprise, her students' behavior and attitude toward the class changed as well. As her students began to experience success, they became less disruptive and more focused on learning.

Her greatest challenge, however, lay ahead. One Friday, when Sharon was about to distribute the weekly quiz to the class, Jeremy appeared at her door. Although he had been on her roll for months, she had seen Jeremy only once in her class this year. On that occasion, she sent him to the office after fifteen minutes of poor behavior, during which he tried to pick fights with others and defied her authority. Sharon quickly picked up a glittery new pencil and handed it to Jeremy with his quiz. Sharon was convinced that Jeremy agreed to take the quiz only to try out this glitzy pencil—all his answers on the quiz were wrong. At the end of the class, Sharon told Jeremy that he could keep the pencil and, if he came to her class on Monday, he would get another surprise.

To Sharon's astonishment, Jeremy did come to her class on Monday. When Sharon handed back the papers to the students, she closely watched Jeremy's face as he received his quiz. At first he looked surprised, but Sharon could not have predicted his next reaction. He proudly showed his grade of "A+" to the other students in the class. Sharon had erased all of Jeremy's incorrect answers and written in correct ones. On a cognitive level, Jeremy probably knew that he did not produce the correct answers on the quiz, yet his emotions allowed him to take ownership of the grade. He was proud—after all, the grade *was* assigned by the teacher.

Jeremy attended school regularly after the reading class that day. His behavior was exemplary, and he worked hard to improve his reading skills. Jeremy's grade in Sharon's class was the first A he had ever received in his school career. His attitude toward school changed not only in Sharon's reading class but also in all his other classes.

At this point, one might question if Jeremy and the rest of the class actually learned anything or if they just felt good about getting "artificial grades." The answer to this question was Sharon's last surprise. After administering the standardized reading comprehension posttest, Sharon found that this class outperformed all other groups of students that she had taught for the previous three years. Sharon had indeed broken the cycle of failure for Jeremy and his classmates.

Upon hearing of Sharon's success, one might think that other teachers in the school would have wanted to try a similar approach to promote an environment of success and trust in their classrooms, especially for the students who appeared to be the most disenfranchised with school. This, however, was not the case. Most of the other teachers thought that giving students answers was not really teaching. Some even became hostile at the thought of a teacher advocating an approach where students were told answers. Sharon's nontraditional approach to breaking the cycle of failure for her students violated their concept of education; they could not see beyond this traditional view of teaching and learning. In their educational paradigm, sometimes referred to as the "banking model" (Claxton, 1990), teachers deposit knowledge into the brains of students, who then give back the information on paper-and-pencil tests and quizzes. Perhaps Sharon was ahead of her time; we now understand the critical role that emotion, especially self-concept, plays in learning.

SELF-CONCEPT AND LEARNING

Today, educators familiar with brain-based learning might agree with Sharon's approach. David Sousa (2001), for example, views self-concept as the most important part of his information-processing model. In this model, information perceived through our senses forms immediate and working memories. If we deem these memories important, they move from our working memory to our long-term storage system and become the basis for our view of the world, a construct that Sousa refers to as the cognitive belief system. It is through our cognitive beliefs that we make sense of events and form decisions about how we interpret our environment. Cognitive beliefs filter and shape our view of the world. A critical component of this view is self-concept, which is a belief about ourselves based on past experiences. If such experiences produced failure in learning, for example, we will then resist accumulating more of this unwanted experience. As we shall see, when emotions struggle with cognition, emotions usually win out.

Traditional cognitive science separated learning from emotion. Learning was thought to involve only the cognitive processes of thinking, reasoning, and intellect, which were viewed as quite separate from the illogical and subjective emotional processes. In recent years, however, scientists have begun to recognize the important role that emotions play in learning. Neuroscientist Joseph LeDoux (1996) argues that emotion and cognition are "separate but interacting mental functions mediated by separate but interacting brain systems." (p. 69)

NEUROBIOLOGY OF EMOTIONS

Such brain systems, identified in chapter 1, are located primarily in the brain's limbic system. LeDoux (1996) explains that when we receive a visual stimulus, the signal goes from the retina to the thalamus, which then sorts the information and sends it to the visual cortex to be processed for meaning in the neocortex. The thalamus also sends the information to the amygdala to determine its emotional relevance. This signal, however, travels from the thalamus to the amygdala quicker than the signal that travels to the neocortex. In contrast to the more complex routing system that occurs as signals travel from the thalamus to the neocortex, the signal that travels to the amygdala moves across a single synapse, sending information to the amygdala 40 milliseconds before the neocortex receives the information. This "quick and dirty" route allows the brain to prepare for an immediate emotional reaction. If the amygdala then senses threat, it triggers the hypothalamus, which in turn activates hormones to prepare the body for action by elevating blood pressure, increasing heart rate, and contracting muscles—a process known as the fight-or-flight response. Our emotional processing system "hijacks" the signal, allowing an emotional response before we are able to produce a cognitive one. This shortcut to the emotional response system thus causes our emotional systems to activate an immediate response before our thinking systems fully register or process the threat (Goleman, 1998).

This emergency-response system propels us to actions to protect ourselves and to respond to emergencies. In evolutionary terms, this quick-response system is critical, because it allows an organism to protect itself from predators. Yet, although fast, this system is not always precise in its assessment. When reacting to fear, our brain responds to sensory information that has not been fully analyzed in the cortex, the thinking center. This explains why we may respond quickly to a perceived threat before we know whether or not the threat actually exists.

LeDoux (1996) explains that it is not easy to return to a relaxed state after a fear response. An emotional reaction such as fear can influence thinking much easier than thinking can affect emotions. After a stress response, the amygdala sends the signal for a flood of hormones, mainly cortisol, to the body. Once secreted into the bloodstream, the hormones can remain in the system for hours. As the heart rate elevates, blood is directed away from the brain's thinking centers to the muscles for quick movement. When cortisol levels are high in the bloodstream, we may become more easily distracted, lose efficiency of working memory, and make more errors. Processing information, especially comprehending what we have read, becomes more difficult.

The effects of long-term stress are troubling. Animal studies have shown a shrinkage of the hippocampus, a center for memory, when the animal is exposed to long-term stress. Acute stress can make us unable to function intellectually, and sustained stress "can have a lasting, dulling effect on intellect." (Goleman, 1998, p. 76) Researchers refer to the chronic diminished capacity to learn due to prolonged stress as "downshifting," a term first coined by Les Hart to describe the process of shutting down thinking to enable the organism to prepare for fight or flight. Geoffrey and Renate Caine (2001) point out that many students in our nation's schools are locked into this downshifted mode of thinking as a result of standard educational practices. Students are thus literally disconnected from their capacity for creativity and learning at high levels. The very institutions charged with developing the creative and higher-level thinking of students are using methods that inhibit this development.

FACTORS OF STRESS THAT INHIBIT LEARNING

Teaching Practices

Teachers have tremendous power to produce or relieve stress for students. Discipline that embarrasses and humiliates students can downshift attention from the brain's thinking centers to its emotional centers. For example, a teacher may use a reprimand with the intent of focusing a child on learning: "Mary, pay attention! You're always looking around instead of focusing on the lesson." Now the child's emotional response system has taken over. Mary is embarrassed and, although she may appear to be attending to instruction, her brain is no longer functioning in its thinking center but rather in its emotional center. The teacher's reprimand, intended to focus Mary on instruction, has actually cut her off from learning, causing her to downshift into a state of humiliation and anger.

Teachers must also be cognizant of the stress created by seemingly benign practices. For example, teachers can create stress for students by issuing unclear directions for performance, either through poorly designed written assignments or indirect, "veiled commands" (Delpit, 1988, p. 289) that disguise a teacher's true intent. Indirect or veiled commands may cause confusion for students, especially those of multicultural backgrounds, who are forced to guess the teacher's intent. For example, a teacher may ask a young child a question—"Is that where your pencil belongs?"—rather than simply giving the child a direction such as, "Please put your pencil in the case." Teachers need to avoid such subtle stress-inducing tactics as calling on learners who have not volunteered, making overt comparisons to higher performing students, employing threats for discipline, using grades and tests as punishments, and failing to communicate directly.

Environmental Conditions

Teachers in urban or poor rural environments understand the negative effects that conditions of poverty have on learning. Many of our students live in homes and neighborhoods where family pressures or violence represent a constant threat. Brain research suggests that threatening environments can cause children to have chemical imbalances (Jensen, 2000). Under chronic stress, the brain not only elevates levels of cortisol, adrenaline, and vasopressin but also inhibits the production of serotonin, a chemical associated with pleasant emotions. With serotonin low and chemicals such as vasopressin high, some students may be prone to impulsive, aggressive, and violent behaviors. Poverty is certainly not the only environmental condition that causes stress for children. Distant or abusive parenting, divorce, financial worries, peer pressures, and a myriad of other environmental stresses can impair children's ability to retain and process information.

School Violence

Incidents of school violence in this country during the past several years have underscored the threats students may face by simply walking through the school entrance. The fear of incidents such as school shootings can produce high stress for students and distract them from the learning process. Such incidents demand that entire communities take responsibility for the climate of the school. Parents, community members, business owners, and policy-makers must become proactive in partnering with teachers and administrators to address threats to the safety of children in school.

Adolescence

Many teachers who work with adolescents believe that their students' emotional centers dominate their cognitive ones. Research supports this supposition: A comparative study conducted by Deborah Yurgen-Todd found differences between teenagers and adults in processing information. Functional MRI images demonstrated that teens processed information more consistently in the amygdala, whereas adults processed the same information in the frontal lobe. Thus, the teens in this study perceived the information through the lens of emotions, while the adults processed it in the brain's cortex, the thinking center. The study concludes that the brain appears to be still maturing emotionally until about age 30 (Howard, 2000). We also know that peer influence peaks during a child's adolescent years, so that those who have most influence on teens are other teens. Although we often joke about the "raging hormones" that our adolescents seem to display, research supports the truth of this supposition. Hormones found in an adolescent's brain during periods of romantic involvement stimulate the hypothalamus, which then emits more hormones into the body (Nunley, 2002). A constant succession of new hormones actually contributes to a teen's employing emotional rather than logical cognitive processes.

Learning Differences, Cultural Differences

Children who display atypical learning styles, whether because of learning disabilities or cultural differences, may experience a disconnection to learning if teaching does not match their instructional needs. Students with learning disabilities often feel the additional fear of rejection from peers that the stigma of special education may bring (Hardiman, 2001). Students whose culture is different from that of the mainstream may withdraw from schooling if classroom experiences fail to acknowledge and support their cultural needs and learning styles (Delpit, 1988; Dixon, Poole, & Hamilton, 2000; Sanders, 1997).

EMOTIONS TO ENHANCE LEARNING

It is critical that educators understand the vital role that emotions play in the lives of young people. Viewing the world through an emotional filter can be troublesome for our students if the emotions are fear and stress. Emotions, though, do not always inhibit learning. Positive emotions can actually contribute to long-term memory and higher-order thinking processes. Researchers have found that laughter, for example, produces chemical changes in the brain and increases the body's production of neurotransmitters, which enhance alertness and memory and boost the immune system (Howard, 2000). Music has also been shown to contribute to a relaxed and alert mental state. In *The Mozart Effect,* Don Campbell (1997) cites research that demonstrates shifts in brain wave patterns when subjects listen to soft classical music. In addition to music, the visual arts, drama, and movement activate the neurotransmitter serotonin, associated with high self-esteem and enhanced cognitive skills (Sylwester, 1994). Emotions, then, are critical for learning, because they give us a more activated and chemically stimulated brain. As Jensen (2000) points out, the more intense the arousal of our amygdala, the stronger the informational imprint, which in turn enhances recall and learning.

Most of us have experienced this phenomenon in our lives. We can usually describe in detail our surroundings when we learned of a catastrophic event, such as the terrorist attack of September 11, 2001. Highly emotionally charged events can imprint a visual image in our brains for an entire lifetime. Similarly, if asked to recall learning activities from our own schooling, most of us would recall experiences such as plays we were in, service-learning activities we completed, or art and musical projects we created. Few of us would describe a paper-and-pencil test or quiz that we took — unless, of course, we failed it!

Thus, establishing a relaxed, stress-free learning environment and connecting learning activities to positive emotions are the initial steps to creating the classrooms our children need for optimum learning.

EMOTIONS AND LEARNING: BRAIN-TARGETED TEACHING STRATEGIES

The following strategies will help to establish an emotional environment conducive to learning:

- Predictability
  - Establish routines that allow students to know what is expected of them as soon as they enter the classroom. For example, many teachers effectively use a short written assignment such as a quick review drill or journal writing as a way to engage students immediately in an independent activity while the teacher engages in "housekeeping" activities such as recording attendance, distributing materials, and so on.
  - Use rituals that are quick and fun to motivate and engage students, such as an inspirational chant or relaxation movements.
  - Assign sections of the board for homework assignments, make-up work, and objectives, so students know automatically where to find information they need.
  - Use standard formats for assignments and projects.

- Personal connection between teacher and students
  - Stand at the door of the classroom and greet students as they enter the classroom. Use each student's name. Smile. Say something pleasant or funny (not sarcastic).
  - Take time to grade students' work and write personal comments. Begin with positive feedback before making corrections.
  - Conduct individual meetings with students outside of class; use an occasional lunch period to dine with a small group of students.
  - Institute a "Student of the Week" program to recognize exemplary or greatly improved performance.
  - Sponsor after-school clubs to get to know students in areas outside the classroom.
- Trust and acceptance
  - Promote self-expression: Let students know that it is safe to express ideas.
  - Promote risk-taking: Show students that we learn from mistakes.
  - Treat students with respect, even when they don't always show respect to others.
  - Treat students fairly; try not to show favoritism to one child while continually correcting another.
  - Explicitly teach peer acceptance, especially for students with learning differences. Conduct class meetings to encourage social acceptance and interaction. Use literature and history to provide instructional materials that demonstrate acceptance of diversity in learning styles and culture (Hardiman, 2001).
  - Begin or end the class period or school day by asking students to write on a slip of paper a kind word or phrase that describes the student they are sitting next to. Put all entries in a box and, when time permits, share them with the entire class.
- Safe environment
  - Establish classroom rules with students' input; focus on respecting others and eliminating bullying.
  - Use task-specific praise to reinforce expectations. For example, rather than telling students, "You are doing a good job," say, "I like the way you are quickly putting away all your supplies."

- Establish multilevel systems of discipline (Jensen, 2000). For example, initially use indirect corrections for a child displaying off-task behaviors. Praise others who are on task: "I like the way all students in these three rows have their eyes on me." Use proximity-control by moving physically to the off-task student, using a gentle touch on the shoulder or a gesture. Obtain the child's attention by altering the activity or the lighting in the room. The next level should involve direct corrections that are explicit: "Jack, your hands belong on your desk." The third level involves providing time outside of class to establish individual rapport and expectations via a written plan for improvement and a system to monitor the plan.
- Control and choice
  - Empower students by allowing them some decision-making in the classroom, such as determining due dates for assignments or choosing classroom displays.
  - Allow students choices in how they demonstrate their understanding of content or concepts. For example, allow them to write an informational essay, construct a model or poster, create a comic strip, make a PowerPoint presentation, or write a creative poem, play, newspaper article, film review, or advertisement.
  - Provide a suggestion box in the classroom and encourage students to give feedback about ways to improve assignments, lessons, or the school environment.
  - Allow students to choose personal learning goals for each unit of study.
- Humor
  - Foster a light-hearted environment by sharing a (tasteful) cartoon or joke with students.
  - Encourage students to share humorous stories and events.
- Music, art, dance, and theater
  - Play soft background music in the classroom to focus attention and influence the growth of connections between brain cells in the cortex (Sousa, 2001).
  - Use the visual arts to activate the brain's right-hemispheric visual-spatial specialization.

- Incorporate movement into lessons to oxygenate the brain and facilitate concentration.
- Allow students to display their creativity through skits, plays, and poetry.
- Begin class sessions with exercises that reduce stress and activate the brain.
- Celebration
  - Celebrate successes with class rituals and rewards.
  - Foster the notion of success as its own reward.

CHAPTER 5

Brain Target 2 (BT-2)
Creating the Physical Learning Environment

A teacher friend contends that a 10-minute walk through a school building just before the beginning of the school day will enable an observer to make a reasonably accurate evaluation of that school's effectiveness, based solely upon its physical environment. A clean, attractive, well-lighted building usually testifies to the quality of learning that takes place there.

The same could be said of an even briefer visit to an empty classroom immediately preceding the arrival of the children. Is the classroom tidy, bright, and colorful? Does a sense of organization, structure, and management pervade the learning space? Does it display evidence of varied, interesting, multicultural learning activities and experiences, and a strong, vital teaching presence? Is children's work neatly displayed? Are measurable learning objectives clearly delineated?

During his first year of teaching, Mr. Johns expended considerable energy creating an inviting learning environment for the first weeks of school. As the school year progressed, however, he allowed cluttered shelves, old displays, faded bulletin board paper, and dog-eared posters to dominate the environment. His busy schedule forced him to regard the unfortunate appearance of his classroom as a low priority among all the other tasks that he performed each day. He has since learned that the physical environment of a classroom is a critical element in teaching and can exert a powerful positive influence on the students who inhabit that space.

In the previous chapter we recognized the importance of establishing an emotional environment to enhance learning for all children. The next component of the brain-targeted teaching model focuses on the importance of the physical environment to support teaching and learning.

Caine and Caine (2001) point out that "context communicates." (p. 71) From corporate offices to stores to media events, physical surroundings are an essential part of the messages that are communicated in our society. Educators must also understand how the physical learning environment speaks volumes to our children, parents, and the community about our philosophy, expectations, and approach to instruction.

In the early 1900s, Maria Montessori recognized the integral role the classroom environment plays in learning. Dr. Montessori developed the concept of the "prepared environment," which includes the use of order, structure, beauty, and atmosphere to enhance children's growth and development (Lillard, 1972). Researchers have since verified that the physical environment does, indeed, affect learning. Bowers and Burkett (1987), for example, found that students who attended schools and classrooms with an optimal physical learning environment performed significantly better in reading, listening, language, and arithmetic. Additionally, students in these carefully planned learning environments, which included controlled lighting, acoustics, as well as a pleasing and orderly use of space, demonstrated better attendance, discipline, and general health than those in less-inviting environments.

THE VISUALLY APPEALING, NOVEL CLASSROOM

Our eyes register about 36,000 visual images per hour, while the retina alone supplies 40% of all nerve fibers that are connected to the brain; 90% of the brain's sensory input is from visual sources (Jensen, 2000). With such enormous visual capacity, the brain continually scans the environment seeking visual stimuli and novelty. The brain's attention will seek out the novel item in a familiar environment. Upon entering a classroom, for example, students frequently notice even minute changes in the environment, such as a teacher's new dress or tie or new colored background paper on a bulletin board.

Teachers can take advantage of the brain's natural propensity to seek novelty by providing visually stimulating environments that support learning objectives and by frequently changing the environment to capture students' attention. Sousa (2001) points out that a classroom environment that lacks novelty and provides the same stimuli month after month "lowers the brain's interest in the outside world and tempts it to turn within for novel sensations." (p. 27)

The studies of Sydney Zentall in the early 1980s confirm the educational impact of the brain's propensity to search for novelty. Zentall (1983) conducted a series of studies to determine the effects of different environmental conditions on behavior and learning by comparing bland, unchanging environments with those that provided novel stimulation. He found that children were generally off-task and out of their seats more often in settings that were familiar. They appeared to seek out additional stimulation through movement around classrooms. Similarly, in studies Zentall conducted with children with attention deficit hyperactivity disorder (ADHD), subjects who were taught in bland classroom environments where they had become "stimulus adapted" (p. 95) were more frequently off-task, out of seats, disruptive, and talkative than subjects taught in environments with novel stimuli. He concluded that children with ADHD are less efficient learners in classrooms where environments and teaching techniques are monotonous and predictable.

It appears then that the brain's appetite for visual stimulation is best met through even subtle changes in the learning environment; classrooms that are bland or lack novelty cause the brain to seek its own visual stimulation. We all know how creative children can be in finding stimulation other than the instructional task at hand! Thus teachers must be committed to changing classroom displays as well as teaching strategies to avoid habituation with the learning environment.

BACKGROUND SOUND

If visually stimulating environments are conducive to learning, one might wonder if the same holds true for auditory stimuli. According to Zentall (1983) the opposite is true for auditory stimuli—too much of it can have detrimental effects on learning. Depending on type, duration, and level, noise often interferes with the brain's ability to process auditory information and can interrupt cognitive processes. Zentall explains that children are less able to control intake of auditory stimulation as opposed to visual stimulation. Too much auditory stimuli impedes the brain's ability to perform complex or unfamiliar tasks.

Although soft background music can help to relax students in the classroom and trigger positive emotions, students generally benefit more from a quiet environment when performing tasks that require complex thinking and concentration, such as engaging in high levels of math or writing an essay. Howard (2000) points out that background music should be used in classrooms only when students are engaged in routine tasks that do not require concentration, as the background can easily become the foreground, thereby impairing concentration.

CLASSROOM LIGHTING

Another aspect of the classroom environment that has received attention is the effect of light on learning. Research generally shows that artificial lighting does affect some aspects of children's performance in the classroom (Fletcher, 1983). Grangaard (1995), for example, found a decrease in off-task behaviors of 6-year-olds by 22% when the classroom environment was changed from white walls and cool-white fluorescent lights to light blue walls and full-spectrum lighting, which most resembles natural sunlight. In a study that examined the effects of natural light on the achievement of over 21,000 students in three school districts, researchers found that students in classrooms with the most natural lighting had from 7% to 18% higher test scores than those in classrooms with the least amount of natural lighting (Kosik & Heschong, 2000). Howard (2000) reports that three elementary schools in North Carolina adopted full-spectrum natural-light environments for their classrooms. The schools reported higher standardized test scores than similar schools with traditional lighting.

Controversy remains, however, as to whether incandescent lamps and "warm" fluorescent lamps, which emit more orange, red, and yellow wave lengths, are more beneficial to students than cool-white fluorescent lights, which emit more blue and green wave lengths (Fletcher, 1983). Although researchers cannot definitively explain how lighting affects learning, many believe that darker classrooms trigger the pineal gland to produce melatonin, which is known to reduce the brain's alertness. Lack of light is also known to produce depression and fatigue; millions of people are diagnosed with seasonal affective disorder (SAD) during the winter months, a time of reduced light.

SMELL

Chapter 1 explained how all sensory perceptions except smell travel first through the thalamus, then to the limbic system for further processing. Olfactory input, however, bypasses the thalamus, taking instead a direct path to the brain's limbic system and memory centers. This short path to our emotional center may explain why smells are able to produce instant vivid memories and emotions from the past. The smell of apple pie baking, for example, may bring detailed visual images of our grandmother's kitchen and strong feelings of comfort and joy. According to John Ratey (2001), researchers have learned that certain odors can alter the heartbeat and blood pressure. Some smells have been shown to have a calming effect, while others are stimulating.

The power of smell to affect the brain's emotional system makes it a powerful complement to learning. In a study designed to determine the effects of pleasant scents on student behavior, Amie Gabriel (1999) dispensed one milliliter of scented oil into a metal oil-burning ring, which was placed on a 60-watt bulb 30 minutes prior to students' entry to the classroom. She applied the scent on two days during the week, then charted the number of times the teacher redirected off-task behaviors of the students throughout the week. She found a 54% reduction of off-task behaviors when students were in the scented environment. Depending on the learning activity, Eric Jensen (2000) suggests the use of scents in the classroom to stimulate or calm students. To increase mental alertness, he recommends odors such as peppermint, lemon, cinnamon, basil, and rosemary. Relaxation and a calm environment are fostered by chamomile, orange, rose, and lavender.

ESTABLISHING AN INVITING LEARNING ENVIRONMENT

Teachers typically have little control over certain aspects of their physical learning environments, such as the type of fluorescent lighting or levels of noise outside the school or classroom. Most teachers, however, can and do control the visual learning climate and the use of classroom space. Based on what we know about how the brain processes the physical world through sensory channels, we can enhance the physical classroom environment through use of the following techniques:

- Establish order in the classroom and engage students in the routine care of the environment. For example, give students tasks at the end of the class or day, like washing boards; picking up stray papers; tidying desk areas, displays, and bookshelves; and watering plants.
- Use horizontal and vertical spaces to add color and beauty and to reflect the current learning unit. Bulletin boards, chalkboards, wall spaces, and shelves should include information and student work that reinforce learning objectives and expectations for student performance, such as class rules and routines.
- Change classroom displays frequently, at least when new learning units are initiated. Use artifacts that reflect the current learning unit.
- Use soft background music to relax students when they are performing routine tasks. Maintain a quieter classroom when students are required to perform tasks that require concentration.
- Use scented oil to establish an atmosphere, with smells such as peppermint to increase alertness or lavender to promote calm.
- Soften harsh fluorescent lighting with lamps; use natural sunlight as much as possible if the room contains windows.
- Create flexible seating arrangements. For example, in classrooms that have individual desks, the arrangement can easily be moved from individual to group seating configurations, depending on the learning task. (In classrooms with tile floors, split tennis balls and put them on the feet of chairs and desks, so they can be moved easily and quietly.)
- Design the learning space to facilitate movement of both teacher and students during the lesson.
- Decorate the classroom with plants, terrariums, or other items to create a homelike atmosphere.
- Display varied examples of students' work.

- Include multicultural themes in classroom displays.
- Post quotations or affirmations that provide inspiration.

Knowing the importance of the physical environment to learning should encourage teachers to focus on creating an exciting, ever-changing classroom. In the brain-targeted teaching model, teachers are encouraged to deliberately plan changes in the physical environment as they establish the objectives for each new learning unit. In the next chapter, which begins our instructional focus, we will set the stage for learning by establishing standards-based learning goals, concept maps, and instructional objectives.

CHAPTER 6

Brain Target 3 (BT-3)
Designing the Learning Experience

As Mr. Johns tackles the daunting task of selecting and planning the first learning unit of the school year, he knows that he must focus initially on providing his students with "big picture" concepts of the content he will teach. His teaching experience has shown him that, if he presents unconnected segments of content to his students, their attention to the lesson and their long-term retention of the information will likely be minimal. He knows that teaching chapter-by-chapter in the U.S. history text and assigning end-of-chapter questions may get his students through the content, but that it will not result in meaningful learning. This teacher has learned an important lesson, supported by brain research: Concepts and skills taught in isolation are meaningless to students.

Neuroscientists tell us that the brain constantly searches for meaning to make sense of the mountains of sensory input it continually processes. The brain's meaning-gathering mechanism occurs through a process known as "patterning"—a way in which the brain categorizes stimuli into concepts that are either familiar or novel, then combines these concepts to create new patterns of thinking and understanding the world (Caine & Caine, 2001). Thus, when students are presented with new information, the brain uses prior knowledge as a filter to establish meaning and relevancy. Brain-targeted teaching supports providing students with "big picture" ideas, then breaking these ideas into connected "concept chunks" that relate students' prior knowledge and understanding to new information to be processed, integrated, applied, and retained.

CONTENT STANDARDS

In applying brain-targeted teaching, Mr. Johns begins planning his school year by charting the content and skills that his students must know and demonstrate command of upon completion of the fifth-grade U.S. history course. He examines national and state social studies content standards and his district's curriculum. Luckily, Mr. Johns works in a school that has a well-defined set of standards based on national, state, and local curriculum priorities. His school's curriculum scope and sequence allows him to see what content his students should have already learned and what they will be expected to know at the end of his course. He examines the reading and writing standards so he can incorporate appropriate expository reading assignments and a variety of related writing experiences into his instructional program. He explores how he can make curricular connections linking history with literature, science, and mathematics as well as the visual and performing arts. He intends to use technology to help his students research topics and apply information to practice higher-order thinking.

Based on curriculum standards, Mr. Johns identifies the content, skills, and processes that students will need to master in the unit. After selecting a general goal for his learning unit, he plans specific objectives that designate what his students will know and be able to do as a result of instruction. He designs strategies that range from direct instruction to the application of knowledge in real-world problem-solving activities. This initial planning targets what students must learn (content, skills, and processes), the educational experiences they will need to acquire this knowledge (instructional strategies), and the methods to be used to assess their learning.

As Mr. Johns designs his first brain-targeted unit, he looks at the *National Standards for History* (1996) for the U.S. history unit entitled "Crisis in the Colonies." In addition, he consults state social studies content standards, which are aligned with the national standards. For this learning unit, the teacher will focus on the state standard: "Students will demonstrate understanding of the causes and course of the American Revolution, the ideas and interests involved in forging the revolutionary movement, and the reasons for the American victory that created the new nation." (Maryland State Department of Education, 2000)

LEARNING GOALS

Mr. Johns now writes a learning goal that describes the overarching theme of the learning unit. His learning goal states: "Students will demonstrate understanding of the important political and economic issues that led the colonists toward revolutionary ideals." He purposely keeps this goal broad to give his students global understanding of the material. Although the teacher will present specific instructional objectives as the unit progresses, he will introduce the lesson by providing only the overall goal of the unit.

This approach, which fosters right-brain holistic learning, aligns with current research. According to Marzano, Pinkering, and Pollock (2001), studies indicate that, if presented with overly specific learning objectives, students tend to focus only on information stated in the objective, resulting in diminished overall learning. Such an approach is comparable to trying to fit puzzle pieces together without ever having seen the whole picture. Conversely, presenting broader goals as an introduction to the learning unit encourages students to engage in holistic thinking. This approach also allows students to personalize learning goals. For example, a student who writes for the school newspaper may want to explore methods used by the colonists to communicate among the states and to describe what role such communication played in forming our national identity; a student who enjoys art could examine how political cartoons influenced colonists' activities. The use of a KWL chart (see Figure 6.1) can help students formulate what they already know regarding the topic (K); personal goals are listed in the column labeled W, which states what students want to learn. At the conclusion of the unit, students state what they learned (L).

CONCEPT MAPPING

After defining the content standards and establishing learning goals, Mr. Johns constructs a "concept map" to develop the key concepts that

What I Know	What I Want to Know	What I Learned

Figure 6.1.   *KWL chart.*

he wants his students to learn. This map is a visual representation of the ideas and major facts that students will acquire during the learning unit (see Figure 6.2).

In their meta-analysis of research on effective teaching, Marzano, Pinkering, and Pollock (2001) cite the use of this type of "nonlinguistic representation" (p. 72) as one of the most effective instructional strategies that teachers and students can use to understand content. Since David Ausubel (1968) first introduced the use of concept maps, research has demonstrated that these organizers significantly enhance learning by helping students understand the conceptual interconnections to which they are exposed during a unit (Dana, 1993; McAleese, Garbinger, & Fisher, 1999; Stice & Alvarez, 1986). Use of such visual representations supports both the left brain's attention to details and language processing and the right brain's holistic, visual-spatial processing style (see Figure 6.3).

As he introduces the learning unit, Mr. Johns presents the concept map to his class and assigns think-pair-share dyads. In this activity, students discuss what they know about each concept on the web. As each dyad offers its ideas to the whole class, the teacher expands the concept

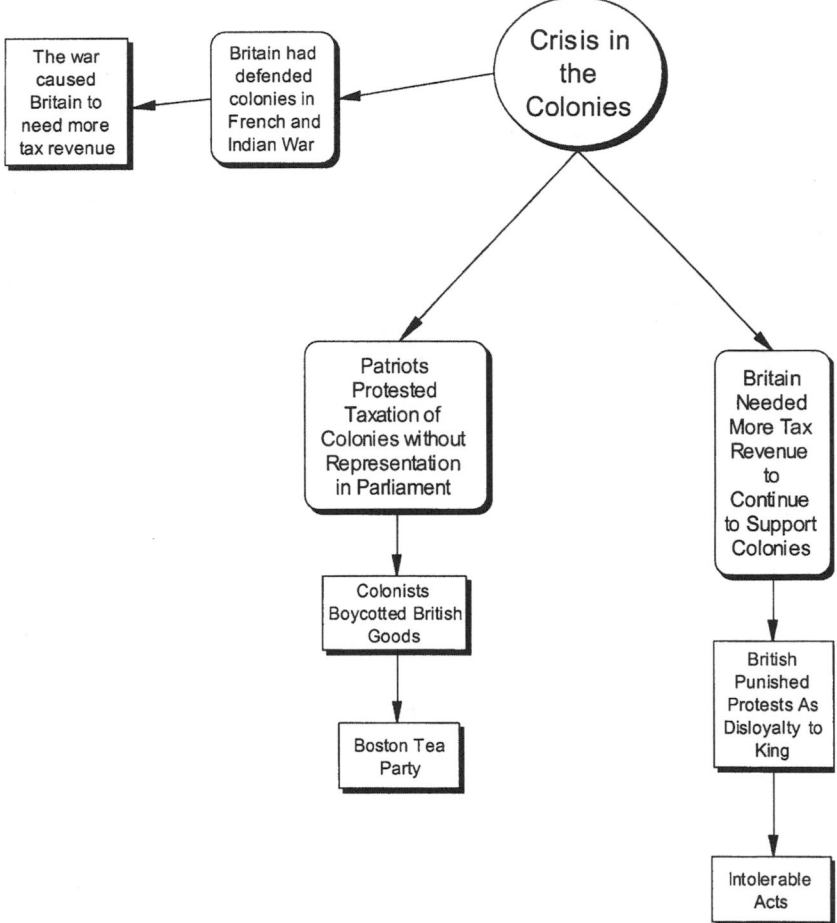

Figure 6.2.   *Concept map.*

map with the students' responses. This activity not only promotes a global introduction of the main concepts of the unit but also helps the teacher determine the students' prior knowledge of the information he is about to teach.

INSTRUCTIONAL OBJECTIVES

Based on the major themes of the unit, Mr. Johns designs instructional objectives that break down major concepts into smaller "content

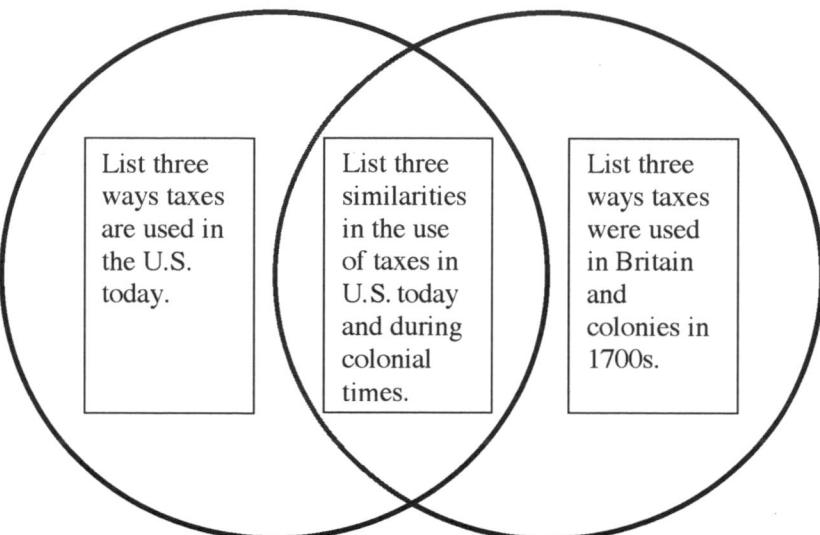

Figure 6.3.   *Venn diagram.*

chunks." His objectives explicitly state what students will know and be able to do as a result of instruction. The "know" component of his objective focuses on content, skills, and processes the students must attain; the "be able to do" component describes how students will demonstrate attainment of that knowledge, skill, or process. For example, a content-based objective might state: "Students will know the differing opinions held by the patriots and loyalists regarding taxation without representation and be able to present an oral and written argument that describes the ideas of each group."

Writing his objectives in this format enables Mr. Johns to be certain that he covers the content and skills that the students must acquire, as delineated in his curriculum scope and sequence. The format also allows him to plan how students will demonstrate their understanding of the content, making sure that he allows students to use multiple modalities to express their thoughts. At the start of the lesson, Mr. Johns will review instructional objectives with his students so they understand clearly what they must know and be able to demonstrate by the end of it. He will use these objectives as a launching point to plan meaningful ways for students to acquire and apply information. He can also use the objectives to help him evaluate how well his students have mastered the material. He will design evaluation strategies, such as oral or written probes, rubrics, quizzes, projects, tests, and performance-based instructional tasks. (For more on evaluation, see chapter 10.)

As a second-year teacher, Mr. Johns has learned the value of taking time to carefully plan and design each unit of instruction. Although the work is demanding, he finds that this planning stage, besides being intellectually challenging and stimulating for him, pays dividends during his teaching of the unit. Advanced planning, including selecting standards, setting goals, and mapping concepts, makes the planning and implementation of daily instructional objectives that much easier. In the long run, a well-planned unit saves time and promotes more effective teaching and learning.

In the next chapters, we will look at what brain research tells us about acquiring knowledge; extending, refining, and elaborating on the learning; and applying its results to real-world tasks.

CHAPTER 7

Brain Target 4 (BT-4)
Teaching for Declarative and Procedural Knowledge

The goal of the teaching and learning process is for students to acquire knowledge and skills that can be used meaningfully throughout their lives. We saw in the previous chapter how learning is improved when students are able to see the "big picture" of a unit of study and to understand how its instructional goals connect with what they already know. In this chapter, we will explore the neurological foundations of learning—how an experience is encoded, processed, stored, and retrieved. We will then examine the next phase of the brain-targeted teaching model: instructional practices that best target what we know about the processes used by the brain to acquire and store information.

THE BRAIN'S MEMORY SYSTEMS

Chapter 1 demonstrated how learning new information causes physical and chemical changes in the brain. As our brain receives a stimulus, the receiving cell sends out neural branches that connect to a neighboring cell, causing the second cell to "fire" upon reception of the impulse or signal from the first cell. As this process continues, more connections among cells are formed, until a neural network or pattern has been established. If this pattern of neural connections continues to receive stimulation, it forms an *engram*, or memory trace (Squire & Kandel, 1999). The more frequently these neural connections are used, the stronger the engram becomes. Thus, repeated firings among cells "hardwire" a memory, strengthening it and making its content easier to retrieve. This process of memory-making, called long-term potentiation (LTP), paves the way for subsequent information to fire along the same neural path. Each time this path is used, it grows stronger by expanding to include neighboring neural cells. Learning takes place when the brain forms such neural networks. As Ratey (2001) states, "[M]emory is the centripetal force that pulls together learning, understanding, and consciousness." (p. 185)

Scientists once believed that memory resided in a particular brain cell or localized group of cells. They concluded that, when those cells died, so did the memory. In recent years, however, neuroscience has shown that memories, rather than being stored in a defined location, are encoded into a network of cells throughout the brain. Stimulation of one of the cells in this neural connection triggers the entire pattern, thus facilitating the retrieval of a memory.

Scientists also know that not all sensory information is encoded in our memory system in the same way. Various factors, including emotions, attention, prior knowledge, and the degree of rehearsal or repeated learning sessions, influence how well we retain information.

Emotions

We know from chapter 4 that emotions can have a profound effect on how information is processed and stored. Events that foster strong emotions, such as the terrorist attacks of September 11, 2001, create "flashbulb memories" that send impulses to multiple parts of the brain, allowing us to remember small details of the experience for many years. Not all stimuli possess this type of emotional charge. Most perceptions slip quickly through our consciousness and are completely forgotten. Some, however, form memories that last a lifetime.

Attention

The degree to which we remember is also affected by the attention we pay to the information when presented or perceived. It should come as no surprise that we remember important or arousing information more than information we regard as trivial or boring. One of the surest ways to capture the attention of students at any age is to introduce novelty into the learning environment.

Prior Knowledge

A third factor affecting memory is our degree of familiarity with the information presented. We are more likely to remember information that connects with pre-existing knowledge. For example, if a teacher uses a well-known sports figure like Michael Jordan to make a point about persistence and hard work, students are more likely to remember her advice than if she references John Adams, our second president, to whom the average student will probably not relate.

Rehearsal

According to researcher Larry Squire (2002), the most important factor determining how well we remember information is the degree to which we rehearse and repeat that information. Moreover, several shorter learning sessions spaced at defined intervals are more effective for remembering information than a single long session. Squire explains that memory storage does not always occur instantaneously upon reception of information. Rather, memories *consolidate* as our brains reorganize, modify, strengthen, or weaken information, based on its presentation and frequency of reinforcement.

TYPES OF MEMORY

As discussed in chapter 2, psychologists identify three types of memory systems: short-term, working, and long-term.

Short-Term Memory

Memories quickly lost after use are called immediate or short-term memories. These memories typically involve information that our brains need to retain briefly, perhaps for only a few seconds or minutes. For example, a teacher may tell her class to turn to page 51 of the textbook to find the definition of a word. Although the teacher hopes that students retain the word's definition, the page number is not important enough to hold in memory for very long. Most scientists believe that, unless repeated and rehearsed, information held in short-term memory is completely lost after being forgotten. Without this loss of short-term memory, our brains, clogged with useless stimuli, would be distracted from focusing on and retaining more important information.

Working Memory

Working memory refers to information that we need for periods longer than a few minutes. It is still a form of temporary storage; we lose this information when we no longer use it regularly. As long as the information receives attention, however, it remains in our working memory. The working memory system serves as a kind of executive assistant, drawing information from long-term memory to be processed when needed.

Baddeley and Hitch (1994) distinguished three types of working memory: the *phonological loop,* which stores auditory information such as words and phonemes; the *visuospatial sketchpad*, which stores visual images and patterns; and the *central executive*, which determines the stimuli to be stored in the working memory system.

Scientists have studied brain activity while subjects were using the working memory system. They found that prefrontal cortical areas of the brain maintained high activity levels when subjects used their working memory systems to engage in delayed-response tasks, i.e., responding to stimuli after a short time delay (Romo, Brody, Hernandez, & Lemus, 1999). Functional MRIs revealed that information retained in working memory activated the prefrontal lobe significantly more if a task included both visual-spatial and verbal activities than if it involved only one or the other (D'Esposito et al., 1995). Cummings (1995) found that people with damage in the prefrontal cortex of the brain had difficulty with working memory, especially if required to process multiple tasks that shifted the focus of their attention from one activity to another.

We know that the working memory system is activated when students memorize information for use on a test, then typically forget it a short time later. Unfortunately, much teaching and learning in our schools draw only upon students' working memories. Brain-targeted teaching, however, promotes the meaningful use of information, so that students develop conceptual frameworks that become part of their long-term memory systems.

Long-Term Memory

Most teachers hope that their teaching will result in students' acquiring knowledge, a process that involves information passing from the short-term to the long-term memory system. Scientists now know that the conversion of a memory from short-term to long-term involves biochemical processes in the hippocampus. Research has shown that forming memories requires proteins to bind to the synapses connecting nerve cells. This process occurs differently depending on whether the information is stored in short-term or long-term memory. Ratey (2001) explains how researchers have recently learned that short-term memory uses proteins currently existing in synapses. However, when information is moved to the long-term memory system, new proteins must be created to bind to the synapse in order to cement that memory in the brain. Scientists believe that the REM sleep period plays a role in helping these connections become etched in memory. It is thought that the brain replays daily experiences during sleep to consolidate them into our long-term memory systems. (Schacter, 1996) Scientists draw a distinction between long-term memory systems, based on whether a memory is part of conscious (explicit) or nonconscious (implicit) learning.

Procedural/Implicit Memory

Procedural, or implicit, memory is the storage of experiences that guide behavior without our awareness that learning is taking place. For example, after many hours of practice, one can become better at hitting a perfect serve in tennis without awareness of the exact movements that have been learned. Procedural memory appears to be stored mainly in the cerebellum and is used in such motor activities as riding a bike, driving a car, and tying shoes. Scientists believe that implicit memory also includes other skills, such as decoding words, which have become automatic through continual repetition. In addition to motor skills, implicit memory includes *priming,* which refers to the ability to improve in the rapid naming of words or objects after repeated presentations. Studies have shown, for example, that when subjects were presented with lists of words or pictures, they could name them faster each time the list was shown. When the lists were interspersed with new words or pictures, the subjects could still name the previously seen items more quickly than the new items. This priming effect was observed even when several weeks had passed between the first and second presentations (Squire, 2002).

Declarative/Explicit Memory

Whereas implicit, or procedural, memory involves nonconscious processes, explicit, or declarative, memory encodes factual information and may be accessed by our conscious awareness. Declarative memory is further categorized into episodic memory, the memory of events, and semantic memory, the recollection of facts.

Episodic memory. As we reflect on events such as performing in a play, taking a driving test, or teaching our first class, we are using episodic memory. According to Squire and Kandel (1999), episodic memory is a record of events that have occurred in our lives, including the when, where, and how of the event. Unlike a video camera, however, our brains do not record events in a linear fashion. Every time we reconstruct an event, the details that we recall may change, sometimes resulting in imprecise or embellished memories.

Semantic memory. A more precise memory system, semantic memory includes facts and information that are part of our long-term experiences. Language symbols, grammar, words and their meaning, and mathematics are all part of our semantic memories. Research has shown that the brain appears to store episodic and semantic memory differently. Several children who experienced damage to the hippocampus, for example, lost the ability to remember simple events that had occurred in their past, yet learned to read and write as well as the other children in the class (Ratey, 2001).

BRAIN TARGET 4 (BT-4): TEACHING FOR DECLARATIVE AND PROCEDURAL KNOWLEDGE

How does brain research relate to classroom practice? While research cannot prove that certain instructional strategies always work, it would be unwise for educators to ignore what neuroscience tells us about how the brain processes, stores, and retrieves information. Current brain research supports the following instructional practices:

- Incorporating emotions into lessons.
- Activating prior knowledge.
- Beginning lessons with "big picture" concepts.
- Allowing time for repeated rehearsals.
- Allowing time between rehearsals for information to "consolidate" into long-term memory.
- Varying learning tasks and providing novelty to sustain attention.
- "Chunking" information by breaking it down into smaller related segments.
- Using mnemonics to remember patterns, rules, or word lists.
- Summarizing information presented through text or lecture.
- Fostering creativity through the use of visual arts, music, and movement.
- Empowering students to make choices.
- Pairing left-brain language tasks with right-brain visual-spatial tasks.
- Integrating technology into the curriculum.

In chapter 6, BT-3 suggested selecting learning goals based on content standards and using strategies such as concept mapping to offer students big-picture concepts. Next, we designed instructional objectives that specified what the students must know and be able to do as a result of instruction. Let us return now to Mr. Johns' classroom and progress to brain target 4, teaching for declarative and procedural knowledge.

Mr. Johns realizes that his students will have to know information from various state content standards in order to pass the social studies assessment at the end of the school year. In his first year of teaching, Mr. Johns observed that his students did not perform particularly well on the curriculum assessment. This perplexed him—he thought he had successfully taught the content. His lectures were well-planned, and his students were mostly successful on his quizzes and unit tests. After reading about brain research, however, Mr. Johns decided to try a different approach.

As he planned the first social studies learning unit for his fifth-graders, Mr. Johns focused on a concept included in state content standards: the issues and controversies between patriots and loyalists that led the patriots to seek independence from Britain. As you may recall from chapter 6, Mr. Johns' first activity was to use a concept map to give his students global understanding of the unit "Crisis in the Colonies." He then planned instructional objectives that stated what students should know and be able to do in each component of the instructional unit.

Let us examine one of Mr. Johns' instructional objectives. It stated: "Students will know the differing opinions held by the patriots and loyalists toward Britain and be able to present an oral and written argument that describes the ideas of each group." Mr. Johns wanted to be certain that his students had enough repeated rehearsals of the material to enable the concept to become part of their long-term memory systems. He also planned to use multiple modalities and to integrate arts and technology into this segment of the unit. He designed the following activities to teach and evaluate the instructional objective:

Activity (BT-1: connecting emotions with learning): Students will discuss the issue of taxation without representation. Mr. Johns told his class that, before they studied the factors leading to the American Revolution, he wanted to solicit their opinions about taxation by discussing a real-life situation in the school. He told students that, because school funds were low, every student in the fifth grade would be required to contribute a sum of money to purchase items that teachers needed in their classrooms. He then told his class that, once the funds were collected, a different class, perhaps the fourth graders, would spend the money in any way they saw fit. Mr. Johns' class discussed whether or not it was fair to collect money for school supplies and examined the inequity of giving another class the privilege of deciding how these funds would be spent. The heated class discussion elicited strong feelings on the part of the students. Mr. Johns concluded the discussion with a reference to the colonists' belief that there should be no taxation without representation.

Activity: Students will read selected sections of the textbook and complete a T-chart identifying the positions of the loyalists and patriots toward Britain. (Refer to Figure 7.1.) Prior to reading the selected text, Mr. Johns examined with his students such textual features as pictures, captions, and bold titles. He reviewed difficult vocabulary as well as major themes in the selection. He explained the use of the T-chart, a graphic organizer used to represent two different elements, and completed one entry with the entire class. Students then individually read the passage and completed the T-chart.

Activity (BT-3: global understanding): In cooperative learning groups, students will complete a concept map that depicts the main

Loyalists	Patriots
1. The British defended the colonies during the French and Indian War. This plunged Britain deeply into debt. It is only right that colonists help to pay for this debt.	1. The colonists believed that the British had no right to tax them because no colonists were represented in Parliament: No taxation without representation. They protested the Sugar Act, the Stamp Act, the Townshend Acts, and the Tea Act.
2. The people in Britain were paying much more in taxes than the colonists were asked to pay.	
3. The colonists were becoming wealthy on trade with Europe. Taxes imposed by the British on the colonies, such as the Sugar Act and the Stamp Act, were only small amounts and were mostly symbolic in order to let the colonists understand that they must pay for the services that Britain provided.	2. The colonists resisted the Writ of Assistance, which allowed British officers to inspect a ship's cargo without giving a reason. Colonists said their right under British law to not be searched without a good reason was being violated.
4. The Proclamation of 1763 forbade colonists from settling land west of the Appalachian Mountains. The Native Americans deserved their land and Britain no longer wanted to bear the expense of defending American settlements.	3. Colonists resisted the "Intolerable Acts" which closed Boston's harbor, forbade Massachusetts colonists from holding town meetings, prevented British customs officers who were accused of crimes from having trials in the colonies, and forced colonists to house British troops.
	4. Colonists believed that the British had no right to tell pioneers that they could not settle land in America.

Figure 7.1.   *T-chart.*

point of view and supporting details for either the loyalists or patriots. Mr. Johns divided his class into six groups. He assigned three groups to summarize the positions of the loyalists and three to summarize the positions of the patriots. Each group completed a concept map using a graphic organizer software program.

Activity (BT-4: repeated rehearsals): Students will use concept maps to depict through artistic expression the views of either loyalists or patriots. Students were offered the choice of displaying information that they summarized on the concept map through the creation of a PowerPoint presentation, poster, cartoon, dramatization, or rap song. Each group gave a presentation, which was followed by student-generated questions and general class discussion.

Activity (BT-4: repeated rehearsals): Students will present an oral argument depicting the views of the patriots and loyalists. Mr. Johns regrouped his students into dyads, consisting of one student from the loyalist group and one student from the patriot group. Each student was responsible for teaching his position to his partner for the oral presentation. Groups presented a three-minute argument depicting both sides of the conflict. The teacher randomly assigned roles for the oral argument and graded the presentations using a three-point rubric (refer to Figure 7.2).

Score	Performance Indicators
3	◉ Presentation clearly and thoroughly demonstrates the viewpoint of patriot or loyalist. ◉ Visual presentation is appealing; performance presentation uses appropriate props and actions. ◉ All members of the group equally participate.
2	◉ Presentation somewhat demonstrates the viewpoint of patriot or loyalist. ◉ Visual presentation is mostly appealing; performance presentation mostly uses appropriate props and actions. ◉ All members of the group participate, but some are more involved than others.
1	◉ Presentation weakly demonstrates the viewpoint of patriot or loyalist. ◉ Visual presentation lacks appeal; performance presentation lacks appropriate props and actions. ◉ Some members of the group participate.

Figure 7.2.   *Group performances: patriot or loyalist point of view.*

Activity (BT-4: reinforcing concept development and writing skills): Taking either a patriot or loyalist position, students will write a persuasive letter to Britain's King George III to recommend a course of action toward the colonies. Finally, to continue to develop his students' writing skills, Mr. Johns assigned the class homework that required them to synthesize their ideas in a letter to King George III. To guide their writing, he gave the students a rubric requiring them to state a clear position, provide supporting details, and conclude with a strong persuasive statement (refer to Figure 7.3).

Answer the questions below. Place in the box "Y" for *yes* and "N" for *no*.

self check /peer check

1. Does the writer thoroughly address the content/topic of the assignment?   ☐ ☐

2. Does the introduction include the topic (main idea) of the writing; does the topic identify a clear position?   ☐ ☐

3. Does the writer use at least 3 details taken directly from the text to support the position?
   Using FEAT("for example" or "according to") helps in citing details from the text.   ☐ ☐

4. Does the writing end with a summary of the main idea and details? Does the summary try to persuade the reader?   ☐ ☐

5. Is the writing organized with a clear beginning, middle, and end, using transition words?   ☐ ☐

6. Does the writing stay true to the form of writing to persuade—that is, does the writer stay focused on the position at all times?   ☐ ☐

7. Does the writer use complete sentences that vary in length and form?   ☐ ☐

8. Does the writer use correct CUPS?
   a. Capitalize the right words
   b. Use words correctly
   c. Punctuate correctly
   d. Spell words correctly   ☐☐☐☐ ☐☐☐☐

Figure 7.3.   *"Writing to persuade" checklist.*

At the conclusion of the unit, Mr. Johns' students not only understood the lesson concepts but had enjoyed the varied activities and the opportunity to choose and create a visual display. Mr. Johns learned an important concept of brain research: Acquiring knowledge requires that information move from students' short-term and working memory to their long-term memory. This is best accomplished if students can manipulate information multiple times in multiple ways. Such repetition of information, which need not include memorization or rote learning, can be exciting and fun for both teacher and students.

The next step of the brain-targeted teaching model explores how knowledge can be extended, refined, and applied meaningfully in real-world settings.

CHAPTER 8

Brain Target 5 (BT-5)
Teaching for Extension and Application of Knowledge

As we learned in chapter 7, teachers can ensure that students acquire declarative and procedural knowledge by providing them with ample opportunities to repeat and rehearse information. Rather than through the use of rote memory tasks, new information is most effectively learned when lessons (a) build on prior knowledge, (b) vary enough to continually attract students' attention, (c) engage the emotions, (d) allow time for knowledge to consolidate in memory systems, and (e) employ multiple modalities through the integration of arts and technology. At this point, if teachers believe that their mission is merely to produce students who can acquire and retain information, they will consider their job done and will be ready to move on to the next topic to be presented. Most effective educators, however, know that the acquisition of content, skills, and processes is only the beginning of a quality instructional program. They realize that good teaching does not stop with the acquisition of knowledge. It also provides students with opportunities to use knowledge meaningfully by developing higher-order thinking and problem-solving skills and by connecting knowledge to real-world applications.

When we extend knowledge by examining it in a deeper, more analytical way, the brain uses multiple and complex systems of retrieval and integration. David Sousa (2001) points out that brain scans demonstrate how different parts of the brain become engaged in the processing of complex thinking and problem-solving tasks. We might better understand this concept by examining the theory of the "modular brain." In recent years, cognitive scientists have proposed that the brain does not process and store information as an integrated whole but rather through distinct components, or modules. When we think of a rose, for example, one module of the brain may be involved in remembering its scent, while another retrieves its visual features; some modules might remember the prick of a thorn or the emotions evoked in receiving roses from a loved one. Neurologist Richard Restak (1994) explains that each brain module connects to others in performing a particular task and that no one system is in control.

The concept of strengthening these connections to enhance learning was first described by Donald Hebb, who suggested that neurons that repeatedly fire at the same time as other neurons are likely to continue firing together in the future. LeDoux (1996) explains this "Hebbian plasticity" theory through the slogan "neurons that fire together wire together." This concept of neural connectivity may be important for many kinds of associative learning (Kalat, 2001). Ron Brandt (1999) explains, for example, that thinking-skills programs directing students to compare and classify familiar concepts require connections among modular brain components. Teachers are therefore promoting connectivity of brain modules when they involve students in instructional activities that allow them to move beyond the mere acquisition of knowledge to engage actively in its extension and meaningful use.

Research has demonstrated that the motor cortex and cerebellum, brain regions originally thought only to control motor functions, are also involved when the brain engages in higher-order thinking that includes the use of memory, language, emotion, and active learning. Ratey (2001) explains that when we analyze, plan, and execute tasks we are using motor functions not only in the performance of the activity but also in the thought processes that precede it. Tasks requiring higher-order thinking, such as creating and executing a plan of action, involve not only the prefrontal and frontal cortex but also the motor cortex. In addition, recent research has identified the cerebellum, previously believed to primarily control automatic movements, as also important to higher-order thinking. Ratey claims that "our physical movements can directly influence our ability to learn, think, and remember." (p. 178)

We may conclude then that neuroscience supports instruction involving the active engagement of students in the learning process rather than lessons promoting only passive learning. Leamnson (2000) warns, however, that merely providing students with "hands-on" activities does not guarantee learning. He suggests that teachers pair physical activities with problem-solving tasks to connect the "acting" modules of the brain, the motor cortex, with the "thinking" modules, the frontal cortex. Such experiences increase memory and learning, thereby modifying brain structure.

Recent studies have demonstrated that active learning not only enhances educational outcomes but also results in chemical changes in the brain. We may recall from our discussion in chapter 2 that Richards et al. (2000), using high-performing readers as a control group, identified boys with learning disabilities and offered them phonics-based reading and enriched science instruction requiring real-world application. Before the intervention, the boys with learning disabilities showed four times as much lactic acid production in the brain as those in the control group, indicating that the brains of the boys with learning disabilities had to work harder to process information. After the intervention, these students, when compared to the control group, demonstrated significantly less lactic acid production, indicating that their brains were exerting less effort during the learning process.

In a similar study, researchers found that the brain showed signs of exerting less effort if subjects learned to perform tasks more efficiently (Bower, 1999). Researchers used functional magnetic resonance imaging (fMRI) to measure blood-flow rates on subjects while they completed learning tasks. As the number of learning trials and task proficiency increased, blood flow slackened. According to Bower, it appears that reinforcement of active learning tasks improves brain efficiency.

It is clear that our understanding of how the brain engages in higher-order thinking is still in its infancy. As Kandel and Squire (2000) point out, "the neuroscience of higher cognitive processes is only beginning . . . requiring new molecular and cellular approaches [that are used] in conjunction with systems of neuroscience and psychological science." (p. 1120) As happened with the human genome, perhaps one day scientists will unravel the mysteries of human consciousness and thought.

THINKING SKILLS FRAMEWORKS

Long before neuroscience tackled the biological basis of cognition, educators recognized the need to provide students with activities that moved them beyond literal levels of learning. In the 1950s, Benjamin Bloom identified six levels of cognition that became the framework for teaching to higher levels of thinking. Bloom's taxonomy begins with the most basic form of learning and progresses to higher-order thinking processes. The six levels include knowledge, comprehension, application, analysis, synthesis, and evaluation. Bloom uses the term *knowledge* to refer to rote recall, labeling, or defining information; *comprehension* indicates the level at which students can summarize and explain information; *application* involves the ability to use information in new settings; *analysis* refers to the ability to understand information by examining its parts; *synthesis* refers to the ability to pull together components to create a product; and *evaluation* is that level at which students can exercise judgments and re-examine biases and points of view.

Similarly, in the 1990s Marzano and others proposed the "dimensions of learning" model based on the "dimensions of thinking" research. Dimensions of learning describes "loose metaphors for how the mind works during learning" (Marzano, 1992, p. 2). The model describes stages similar to Bloom's taxonomy, from the initial teaching for acquiring knowledge to activities that require higher levels of extension and application.

Despite most teachers' familiarity with these hierarchical thinking frameworks, some would argue that little has changed in American classrooms during the past 40 years, because many instructional and assessment strategies require students to demonstrate only their acquisition of knowledge. According to Sousa (2001) many teachers admit that barriers exist hindering consistent use of higher-level learning activities in the classroom. Such activities, besides requiring teachers to devote extra hours to planning, also consume more instructional time. Many teachers worry that the additional time spent helping students to extend and apply knowledge will prevent them from completing the required scope of the curriculum. They feel pressured to cover the growing number of content standards while still incorporating into the curriculum the latest requirements of the school district, such as character education, service learning, and violence and drug prevention. Yet, as we have learned from the cognitive sciences, true learning occurs best when teachers require students not merely to acquire knowledge but to use it actively and meaningfully in real-world contexts. Such activities, which target both left-hemispheric language processing and right-hemispheric visual-spatial processing, motivate and stimulate students and promote creative thinking by encouraging the integration of the arts, technology, music, movement, dance, dramatizations, experiments, and inventions. The following examples demonstrate strategies that teachers can use to allow students to extend learning and knowledge in meaningful ways. In brain target 5, teachers design activities that guide students to:

- compare and contrast elements;
- classify information;
- engage in inductive thinking—drawing general conclusions from specific parts;
- engage in deductive thinking—making predictions based on generalizations;
- analyze error patterns;
- analyze perspective;
- promote creative thinking through the visual and performing arts;
- create metaphors and analogies;
- elaborate, analyze cause-effect patterns;
- conduct investigations;
- design experiments;
- solve problems using real-world contexts.

BRAIN TARGET 5: TEACHING FOR THE EXTENSION AND APPLICATION OF KNOWLEDGE

It is now time to catch up with Mr. Johns' classroom and see how he is implementing brain target 5. In chapter 6, we examined Mr. Johns' learning goal (BT-3) for the unit "Crisis in the Colonies," which stated that his students will demonstrate understanding of the important political and economic issues that led the colonists toward revolutionary ideals. He broke this goal down into instructional objectives, including the objective that we analyzed in chapter 7, "students will know the differing opinions held by the patriots and loyalists toward Britain and be able to present an oral and written argument that describes the ideas of each group." The activities supporting this objective offered the students a number of diverse tasks to cement the information into their long-term memory systems (BT-4). Mr. Johns will now extend his students' understanding by designing activities that will allow them to explore the information in new ways (BT-5).

Activity: Using the Internet, students will find political cartoons that describe the patriot or loyalist point of view. This activity, besides requiring students to use technology, also asks them to apply higher-order analytical skills. Additionally, they will learn the difference between primary and secondary source documents. The teacher will explain how to use search engines to retrieve historical documents.

Activity: Students will write a paragraph that describes the symbolism of various features of a cartoon and explains how these features support either the patriot or loyalist position. This activity requires students to analyze details of a political cartoon and synthesize information from the document to demonstrate global understanding of the concepts it depicts.

Activity: Students will assume the role of King George III and write a sentence that creates an analogy and one that creates a metaphor describing the behavior of the patriots during the Boston Tea Party. They will evaluate their writing using a student-created rubric. This activity promotes the use of alternate points of view and allows students to use language structures to describe historical events. In cooperative learning groups, students will apply their knowledge of analogy and metaphor to create a grading rubric. They will then evaluate each other's analogy and metaphor. Mr. Johns will grade each group's rubric to determine if it demonstrates understanding of these two language structures.

Activity: Students will determine how taxes are spent in the United States today and list seven benefits that federal taxes provide or support. They will develop a pie chart to demonstrate the percentage of the federal budget that each benefit requires. As a real-world application, this activity requires students to apply research skills, analyze data, and create a graphic presentation of the data. Students will also employ technology skills to research the information using the World Wide Web.

Activity: Students will complete a Venn diagram comparing and contrasting tax benefits in colonial times with tax benefits in the United States today. Students will research how the British government spent tax money collected from British citizens and colonists and compare this information to the data they collect on U.S. tax expenditures.

Activity: Choose a modern-day situation that demonstrates boycott or protest against an action of the government, such as the bus boycott in Montgomery, Alabama, after the arrest of Rosa Parks, the boycott of grapes led by Cesar Chavez, or the protests and burning of draft cards during the Vietnam War. Write and illustrate a report comparing and contrasting the modern protest with the patriot boycott against British tea. Mr. Johns will assign this activity as a long-term project that students will research and write outside of class. He will teach his students the steps necessary to conduct research and write a report, including taking notes on index cards, constructing an outline, writing the first draft, editing, engaging in peer review, revising, and completing the final draft. He will collect and review products from each step of the process.

Mr. Johns combines the student-directed activities that he has designed with direct instruction using traditional formats, such as lecture, textbook readings, films, and discussion. He uses his knowledge of his students' instructional levels and academic needs to determine which activities they can complete independently and which require his direct assistance and support. He also uses strategies such as class-wide peer tutoring to assist students with special needs who may require extra support. Mr. Johns individualizes learning objectives and provides extended time to accommodate these students.

The next chapter describes brain target 6, evaluating instruction. We shall see that evaluation for Mr. Johns has expanded beyond end-of-chapter tests to include a variety of strategies and choices.

CHAPTER 9

Brain Target 6 (BT-6)
Evaluating Learning

Although evaluating student learning is the last stage of the brain-targeted teaching model, we mustn't be fooled into thinking that evaluation happens only after instruction has occurred. Evaluating learning is embedded into every stage of this model, becoming the teacher's constant "dipstick," as it were, in recognizing that learning has taken place.

In traditional teaching, a teacher typically evaluates instruction by giving students quizzes during a unit, with a culminating test at the end. These tests and quizzes usually require students to select responses, as in multiple choice items, and sometimes to construct a response, as in an essay question. Occasionally, the teacher also assigns supplementary activities, such as projects, research papers, and in-class assignments, which will also be assessed. The combined scores of such assessments are then used to determine students' grades. Sound familiar? Such an approach, while common among many classroom teachers today, does little to inform instruction or enhance learning. It also defies what we know about the brain's natural learning systems.

While it is certainly a valid instructional practice to assess content and skills for the purpose of assigning grades, evaluation that supports effective teaching practices, based on our understanding of brain research, must accomplish the following:

- provide students with immediate, frequent, and relevant feedback about their performance;
- allow the teacher to make better instructional decisions;

- offer continual information relative to individual student performance;
- foster authentic performance assessment.

FEEDBACK: IMMEDIATE, FREQUENT, RELEVANT

Marzano, Pickering, and Pollock (2001) identify the practice of giving students appropriate feedback as one of the most effective research-based strategies to improve student achievement. In their book *Classroom Instruction that Works: Research-based Strategies for Increasing Student Achievement,* they cite the results of a meta-analysis of eight studies with effect sizes of .90 or greater, indicating that students who received relevant feedback performed significantly better on achievement measures than students who did not receive the feedback.

The research also demonstrated that timely rather than delayed feedback is more effective for reinforcing or correcting learning. It does not take a meta-analysis of research to understand this point—ask students how they feel about receiving a grade for a test or essay several weeks (or longer) after it was submitted. Most will tell you that their interest in how they performed on a task was greatest shortly after they completed it. If too much time passed, students usually reported diminished interest in their performance and in the material assessed because they had become focused on new materials and tasks. Clearly, teachers and administrators should regard appropriate feedback to students as an instructional priority. Thus, it is unwise for teachers to put off grading and returning students' work and equally unwise for school or central-office administrators to continue to place ever-growing burdens of non-instructional paperwork on teachers without additional time or support.

Research also shows that the nature of the feedback makes a significant difference in student performance. Studies demonstrate that learning is enhanced when students are given specific feedback that is corrective in nature—that is, information that tells them why a response is not correct or how they can improve performance. This is especially important when grading essays. Teachers can help students to improve their writing when they offer relevant feedback not only about content but also about structure, organization, vocabulary, and language usage.

INSTRUCTIONAL DECISION-MAKING

Besides providing relevant feedback to students, evaluating instruction allows teachers to understand to what degree students are mastering educational outcomes and how to adjust instruction accordingly. Most educators agree that teachers shouldn't wait until they administer an end-of-unit test to determine whether or not their students have met educational outcomes. By regularly measuring students' performance, teachers will know during or after each lesson the degree to which learning has taken place and will be able to make appropriate adjustments to instructional plans based on that performance.

As an example, let's examine this process as it occurs in Mr. Johns' lesson about patriots and loyalists. The initial objective stated, "Students will know the differing opinions held by the patriots and loyalists toward Britain and be able to present an oral and written argument that describes the ideas of each group."

As we saw in chapters 7 and 8, Mr. Johns used this objective to design instructional activities that also served as a type of sub-objective to measure student performance. For example, you may recall that one of Mr. Johns' initial activities stated, "Students will read selected sections of the textbook and complete a T-chart identifying the positions of the loyalists and patriots toward Britain" (refer to Figure 7.1). After his students completed this task, Mr. Johns collected the T-charts to determine how well the students were able to obtain information from the text. By evaluating the T-charts, he was able to ascertain whether or not each child had comprehended the text well enough to identify main ideas and relevant details (i.e., loyalist and patriot positions toward British rule). If most students had successfully completed the T-chart, Mr. Johns knew that they were ready for the next activity, which included a cooperative learning task to develop a concept map. On the other hand, if a majority of students had struggled with the T-chart assignment, Mr. Johns knew he would need to use the text and other supplementary materials to teach the concepts directly.

INDIVIDUAL STUDENT PERFORMANCE

Continuous evaluation of student performance also allows teachers to know which students require adjustments to instructional activities and how best to adapt learning tasks to accommodate these individual needs. Every teacher knows that all students do not learn in the same way and at the same rate. Howard Gardner's work on multiple intelligences demonstrates that, although some students' processing strengths may favor traditional styles of learning, such as verbal/linguistic or logical/mathematical, others may incline toward different learning styles, such as bodily/kinesthetic, musical/rhythmic, visual/spatial, or naturalist. Some students work better in interpersonal/social groups, while others benefit from intrapersonal/introspective types of learning activities. By assigning a variety of learning activities that tap into different learning styles, and by monitoring individual student performance, teachers can teach most effectively to the strengths and needs of each student. Additionally, students with Individualized Education Programs or 504 Accommodation Plans require teachers to design and implement instructional adjustments based on diagnosed needs. Individual student portfolios are another excellent way to track how all students, especially those with disabilities, are progressing in terms of both curriculum and skills development. Maintaining writing folders throughout the school year can help both teacher and student to evaluate progress.

Returning to Mr. Johns' lesson, we see that by evaluating students' performance on the T-chart, the teacher could determine which students completed the independent reading and writing task with ease and which students required additional assistance. When assigning students to the next activity, which required them to work in cooperative learning groups to complete a concept map, he could pair students who struggled with the reading/writing task with those who demonstrated greater mastery of the assignment. Additionally, he could monitor the performance of the students with special needs to be certain that they were able to perform successfully within the group. Those who continued to have difficulty understanding the concepts might benefit from individual teaching through peer coaching or after-school help. Mr. Johns could also extend the time allowed for students with special needs to complete the tasks.

Mr. Johns' objectives allow all students to demonstrate understanding of the content in multiple ways. For example, in the next activity of the unit, Mr. Johns states that "students will use concept maps to create a visual display depicting the views of either the loyalists or patriots." He offers students choices in how to create the display, including PowerPoint presentations, posters, cartoons, skits, or writing and performing a rap song. To guide the preparation of this activity, Mr. Johns gives students a rubric that he will use to evaluate their learning (refer to Figure 7.2). Besides offering students opportunities for creativity and fun, this activity allows them to use their preferred learning styles to demonstrate command of content.

Mr. Johns' next activity also accommodates individual learning styles, by requiring each student to present an oral argument depicting the views of patriots and loyalists. Mr. Johns is then able to determine students' mastery of the objective through oral responses, which adds variety to the lesson and accommodates students with disabilities who may have difficulty performing reading and writing assignments yet demonstrate strengths in oral expression. Mr. Johns supplies his students with a four-point rubric (see Figure 9.1) to provide structure and direction as they prepare their oral argument.

AUTHENTIC PERFORMANCE ASSESSMENT

We have reviewed how evaluation of student performance not only provides information for end-of-quarter grading but also enhances learning by giving students timely and appropriate feedback. We will now consider how assessments can mirror what we know about how the brain learns.

We know that learning is enhanced when students are actively involved in meaningful and relevant activities that utilize the brain's centers for higher-order thinking. Activities that require active participation of the learner in higher-order thinking tasks, as in performance-based instruction, can blur the line between teaching and assessment. In performance-based teaching, students typically solve real-world problems through such activities as decision-making, investigation, experimental inquiry, problem-solving, and invention (Marzano et al.,

Score	Performance Indicators
4	◎ Student is thoroughly prepared to take either position of patriot or loyalist. ◎ Student is able to provide four details to support designated position. ◎ Student thoroughly summarizes position at the beginning and end of presentation. ◎ Student consistently uses convincing language, clear speech, and maintains eye contact with audience.
3	◎ Student is somewhat prepared to take either position of patriot or loyalist. ◎ Student is able to provide three details to support designated position. ◎ Student summarizes position at the beginning and end of presentation. ◎ Student mostly uses convincing language, clear speech, and often maintains eye contact with audience.
2	◎ Student is prepared to take one of the positions of patriot or loyalist. ◎ Student is able to provide two details to support designated position. ◎ Student weakly summarizes position at the beginning and end of presentation. ◎ Student seldom uses convincing language, clear speech, and rarely maintains eye contact with audience.
1	◎ Student is unprepared to take either position of patriot or loyalist. ◎ Student is able to provide only one detail to support designated position. ◎ Student fails to summarize position at the beginning and end of presentation. ◎ Student fails to use convincing language, clear speech, and does not maintain eye contact with audience.

Figure 9.1.   *Rubric for oral presentation.*

1992). They display their knowledge by developing products such as charts, graphs, and written or oral presentations.

What is the difference, you may ask, between performance-based teaching and performance assessment? The distinction rests simply on the degree to which the teacher is involved in the activity. For example, when a teacher is actively involved directing students through the stages of a science experiment, it would be considered performance-based instruction; on the other hand, when students perform this experiment independently, and the task is evaluated using a rubric, it becomes an assessment. Performance-based instruction demonstrates the fine line that exists between teaching and testing.

Mr. Johns wants his students to use their knowledge of the reasons for the conflict between the British and the colonists. They have learned to take both positions, so they can understand and articulate that multiple points of view exist in most conflicts, a higher-order cognitive skill. To apply the skill of taking multiple points of view as well as to develop the skill of writing persuasive arguments, the teacher required students to assume either a patriot or loyalist position and write a letter attempting to persuade King George III to initiate a particular course of action. Mr. Johns evaluates this assignment using a scoring checklist that facilitates not only teacher assessment but also self and peer review of persuasive writing skills (refer back to Figure 7.3).

The next activity asks students to apply their knowledge of historical content to a present-day situation. Mr. Johns asks students to investigate how taxes are spent in the United States today and compare this information to how the British used tax revenues collected from the colonists. The teacher creates a Venn diagram scoring key to guide students' performance and evaluate their work (see Figure 9.2).

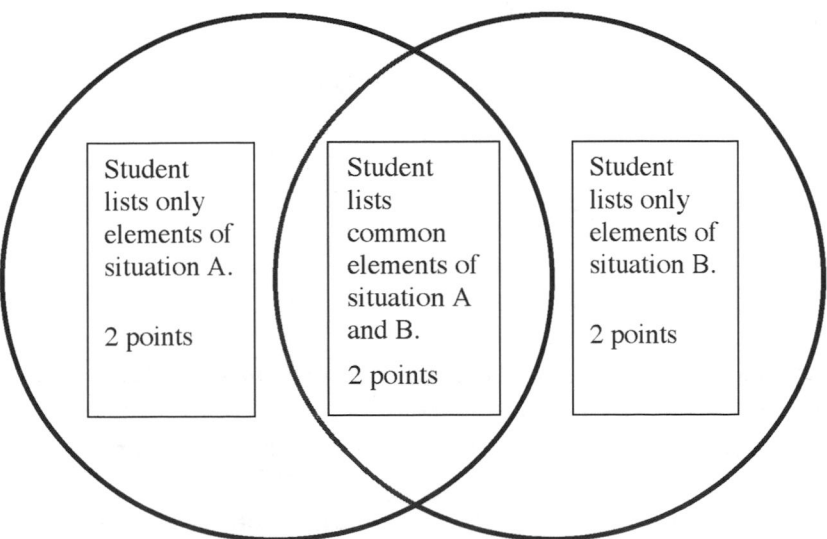

Figure 9.2. *Scoring key for Venn diagram.*

As a long-term research assignment, Mr. Johns' students compare a modern-day boycott with the colonists' boycott of tea. The teacher uses an analytic scoring rubric, such as the following example, to provide his students with guidance with their writing and to assign them grades:

Analytic Writing Scoring Rubric

Element 1: The student responds to the compare/contrast prompt.

4. The writing thoroughly compares and contrasts the two elements.
3. The writing generally compares and contrasts the two elements.
2. The writing vaguely compares and contrasts the two elements.
1. The writing does not compare and contrast the two elements.

Element 2: The writing includes main idea specific to the writing prompt.

4. The student begins a paragraph or report with a main idea statement that synthesizes specific and purposeful information from sources.
3. The student begins a paragraph or report with a main idea statement that synthesizes general information from sources.
2. The student begins with a main idea statement that vaguely synthesizes sources.
1. The student does not begin the paragraph or report with a clear main idea statement.

Element 3: The writing includes supporting details specific to the main idea and appropriately cites sources.

4. The student uses specific details from sources that are appropriately cited.
3. The student uses general details from sources that are generally cited appropriately.
2. The student uses general information from sources that are sometimes cited appropriately.

1. The student does not use sufficient information from sources and does not cite appropriately.

Element 4: The writing ends with a concluding statement/synthesis of the paragraph or report.

4. The student concludes the writing with a statement or paragraph that accurately and purposefully summarizes/synthesizes the main idea and details, and extends the writing by including information from other sources or general background knowledge.
3. The student concludes the writing with a statement that adequately summarizes/synthesizes the main idea and details.
2. The students concludes the writing with a statement that provides a limited summary/synthesis.
1. The student does not adequately summarize/synthesize the writing.

Element 5: The writing is organized and sequenced using transition words.

4. The writing reflects an organizational plan that clearly reflects a beginning, middle, and end. The ideas are accurately sequenced. The writing is held together with transition words and statements.
3. The writing reflects a general organizational plan.
2. The writing reflects limited organization.
1. The writing lacks general organization.

Element 6: The writing addresses a point of view true to form (writing to inform, persuade, express personal ideas) and the intended audience.

4. The student provides relevant information that consistently stays true to the form of writing and consistently addresses the intended audience.

3. The student provides information that generally stays true to the form of writing and addresses the audience.
2. The student in a limited way is true to form and addresses intended audience.
1. The student does not write in a way that is generally true to the form of writing and does not address the intended audience.

Element 7: Sentences are varied to engage and sustain the interest of the reader; sentences include content-specific language.

4. The student consistently uses language choices, style, and tone to enhance the text, including varying the sentence length and structure.
3. The student frequently uses language choices, style, and tone to enhance the text, including varying the sentence length and structure.
2. The student sometimes uses language choices, style, and tone to enhance the text, including varying the sentence length and structure.
1. The student rarely or never uses language choices, style, and tone to enhance the text, including varying the sentence length and structure.

Element 8: CUPS (capitalization, usage, punctuation, and spelling) are appropriate for age/stage of writer.

4. The student consistently demonstrates correct capitalization, usage, punctuation, and spelling.
3. The student frequently demonstrates correct capitalization, usage, punctuation, and spelling.
2. The student sometimes demonstrates correct capitalization, usage, punctuation, and spelling.
1. The student rarely demonstrates correct capitalization, usage, punctuation, and spelling.

It is clear that, built into Mr. Johns' learning unit, there are activities that allow him to continually evaluate student performance. He uses this data to give students immediate feedback, to accommodate learning styles and needs, and to enable students to demonstrate their understanding of higher-order thinking skills using real-world applications. For some activities in the lesson, Mr. Johns uses rubrics to give students numerical scores; for other activities, he provides students with feedback without assigning formal grades. For example, he grades the oral argument and the persuasive letter using scoring rubrics. On the other hand, he may only review other activities, such as the creation of concept maps, to be certain that students have understood the concepts and provide written comments rather than numeric grades on students' work. Mr. Johns also extends learning beyond his class by assigning some activities in the learning unit for homework. His learning unit (see chapter 10) designates which activities he believes can be extended to homework for completion and practice. Finally, Mr. Johns returns to the KWL chart that his students completed at the start of the lesson. He allows students to evaluate their own learning by completing the last column (L), indicating what they believe they learned from the unit, both academically (content, skills, and processes) and socially (working effectively on their own, in pairs, and in groups).

At the end of his teaching unit, Mr. Johns has already evaluated his students on a wide array of tasks that used multiple modalities and required skills in oral and written expression. Does he still administer an end-of-unit test? Perhaps. But, because his students have had multiple experiences to help them acquire, extend, and use the concepts in the unit, he knows, in advance, that they will be able to apply that learning to future tasks beyond his own classroom.

CHAPTER 10

Brain-Targeted Learning Units

I hope you have enjoyed walking through the six stages of the brain-targeted teaching model. I also hope you will find the information useful as you begin to plan or support research-based effective instruction in your own classroom or school.

At Roland Park Elementary and Middle School in Baltimore, Maryland, the use of this model has resulted in seven years of continuous improvement in our state standards-based performance assessment and has made instruction come alive. Teaching that focuses on applying knowledge to meaningful tasks supports what neuroscience tells us about how the brain learns. What better reason to make the stages of brain-targeted teaching a part of what teachers do every day in our nations' schools?

To help get you started with planning your own brain-targeted teaching, I have included learning units designed by teachers from Roland Park and other schools. We'll start with good old Mr. Johns' American history unit that we have been following throughout the book. Then we'll look at a series of other learning units, including an exciting trip around the world with Cinderella for first-grade students, a multidisciplinary study of the life of Leonardo da Vinci for ninth graders, a third-grade science lesson that demonstrates the development of a plant from a seed, an examination of Shakespeare's *Julius Caesar* for seventh-grade students, and a high school lesson focused on the application of Spanish. Feel free to use and modify these plans.

BRAIN-TARGETED LEARNING UNIT: AMERICAN HISTORY

Title: Crisis in the Colonies
Grade Level: 5
Time Frame: 1–2 weeks
Social Studies Standard: Demonstrate understanding of the causes and course of the American Revolution, the ideas and interests involved in forging the revolutionary movement, and the reasons for the American victory that created the new nation.
Writing Standard: Demonstrate the ability to write persuasive arguments that reflect multiple points of view.
Reading Standard: Demonstrate the ability to read a variety of texts for global understanding and interpreting details.

Brain Target 1: Emotional Connection

Activities:

1. Connect students to concept of taxation without representation. Give them real-life scenario to experience how it feels to pay taxes without having the ability to choose how the taxes would be spent. Tell them they would be required to bring in money for classroom supplies, but another grade would determine which supplies to purchase. Discuss how they felt about taxation without representation.
2. Include arts integration by allowing students to choose how to depict concepts taught during the lesson.
3. Offer assistance to students with special needs; use multiple modalities to demonstrate learning.
4. Allow students to evaluate their own cognitive and social learning on a KWL chart.

Brain Target 2: Physical Environment

Activities:

1. Arrange desks in clusters for cooperative activities.
2. Display pictures of leading figures that students will read about during the lesson, such as King George III, John Adams, Samuel Adams.

3. Display pictures of the Boston Tea Party.
4. Display student products.

Brain Target 3: Big-Picture Activity

Learning Goal: Demonstrate understanding of the major factors that led patriots to pursue independence from Britain.

Activities:
   1. Students review the concept map demonstrating major themes of the lesson. In "think-pair-share" dyads, they brainstorm what they know about each concept on the web. Each group offers ideas to the class. As they respond, the teacher adds their ideas to the concept map.
   2. Each student completes a KWL chart, indicating what they already know about issues of disagreement between the colonists and British that led to the American Revolution and what they want to learn during the unit.

Brain Target 4: Declarative and Procedural Knowledge

Learning Goal: Students will know the different opinions held by the patriots and loyalists toward Britain and be able to present an oral and written argument that describes the ideas of each group.

Activities:
   1. Students discuss the issue of taxation without representation.
   2. Students read selected sections of the textbook and complete a T-chart identifying the positions of the loyalists and the patriots toward Britain. (Class work or homework)
   3. In cooperative learning groups, students complete a concept map that depicts the main point of view and supporting details for the ideas of either the loyalists or patriots.
   4. Students use information from concept maps to create a visual display or performance. (Class work or homework)
   5. Students present oral arguments depicting the view of the patriots and loyalists.
   6. Students take the position of either a patriot or loyalist and write a letter to King George III to persuade him to take a certain course

of action toward the American colonies. (Class work or home-work)

Brain Target 5: Extension and Application of Knowledge

Learning Goal: Students will know the issues facing the colonists prior to the American Revolution and be able to describe the points of view of colonists and the British using political cartoons and student-created metaphors and analogies.

Activities:
1. Using the Internet, students find political cartoons that describe the patriot or loyalist point of view toward British activities prior to the American Revolution.
2. Students write a paragraph describing the symbolism of various features of a political cartoon and explaining how these features support either the patriot or loyalist position. (Homework)
3. Students assume the role of King George III and write one sentence that creates an analogy and one that creates a metaphor describing the behavior of the patriots during the Boston Tea Party.

Learning Goal: Students will know how taxes support governments and compare how the United States uses tax dollars today with how Britain used tax dollars in colonial times.

Activities:
1. Using the Internet, students research how taxes are collected and spent in the United States today and list seven benefits that federal taxes provide or support. (Homework)
2. Based on class discussion and written sources such as the textbook and other historical documents, students determine how the British government collected and spent taxes garnered from British citizens and colonists.
3. Students complete a Venn diagram comparing the general use of U.S. taxes today with the use of British taxes in colonial times.
4. Students choose a modern-day situation that demonstrates boycott or protest against an action of the government, such as the bus

boycott in Montgomery, Alabama, after the arrest of Rosa Parks; the boycott of grapes led by Cesar Chavez; or the protests and burning of draft cards during the Vietnam War. Students write and illustrate a report comparing and contrasting one modern-day protest with the patriot boycott of British tea.

Brain Target 6: Evaluating Learning

1. Review the T-chart and reteach if needed; determine how to group students for cooperative learning activity.
2. Use rubric to evaluate student presentations.
3. Use rubric to evaluate oral arguments.
4. Use writing checklist to evaluate persuasive letters.
5. Use anchor paper to allow students to self-grade and correct paragraphs.
6. Have students create rubrics and self-grade sentences.
7. Use scoring key to evaluate Venn diagram.
8. Use rubric to evaluate research project.
9. Have students self-evaluate using KWL chart.
10. Administer end-of-unit test.

Materials: textbook and supplementary reading materials, Internet-connected computers, "Inspiration for Kids" software, political cartoons, overhead projector.

AROUND THE WORLD WITH CINDERELLA

Teachers: Kathy Rivetti, Kelly Rietschel, Catherine Gearhart

We each brought a varying perspective to the curricula that, over time, we have combined into this cohesive unit. In the past, geography, literature, and writing were taught in isolation. By linking the objectives of each discipline, we have created an exciting unit which not only accomplishes the academic goals but enhances the learning environment. The brain-targeted teaching model has enabled us to organize activities into a formalized unit plan. This model is a strong tool for teachers to develop interdisciplinary curricula and creative approaches to teaching and learning.

Originally, world geography was taught in September, Cinderella stories in November, and writing friendly letters in January. Once we realized the connections among these activities, it was easy to rearrange their scope and sequence. Now we teach the unit at the beginning of the school year, using Cinderella stories to create the emotional connection to learning about world geography. Pretending to travel from continent to continent, stamping our passports along the way and writing postcards home from each stop, taps into the imaginations of our first-graders. They are having so much fun listening to fairy tales, singing songs, looking at artifacts, and reading about animals that they hardly notice they are learning about maps, climates, environments, cultures, elements of a fairy tale, settings, and the format of a friendly letter. This awareness, however, does occur, and they become quite proud of themselves for their accomplishments!

BRAIN-TARGETED LEARNING UNIT: GLOBAL AWARENESS AND FAIRY TALES

Title: Where in the World Is Cinderella?
Grade Level: 1
Time Frame: 3–4 weeks
Geography Standard: Use geographic concepts and processes to examine the role of culture, technology, and the environment in the location and distribution of human activities and spatial connections throughout time.
Literature Standard: Interpret and analyze the meaning of literary works from diverse cultures and authors by applying different critical lenses and analytic techniques.
Writing Standard: Produce informative practical, persuasive, and narrative writing that demonstrates an awareness of audience, purpose, and form, using stages of the writing process as needed (i.e., prewriting, drafting, revising, editing, and publishing).

Brain Target 1: Emotional Connection

Students love fairy tales. They will form an emotional connection with geography content skills by following Cinderella around the world.

They will enjoy traveling around the world using their personal passports and sending postcards home.

Brain Target 2: Physical Environment

Activities:

1. Create displays of unit-related artifacts.
2. Arrange desks for cooperative groups.
3. Display large world map and globe in classroom.

Brain Target 3: Big-Picture Activity

Learning Goals: Students will know through literature how people from different cultures, climates, and geographic locations live. Students will know continents, oceans, and landforms and be able to locate each on a world map, and will know elements of a globe/map and be able to identify and use them to describe areas in the world. Students will know geographical climates and be able to identify and describe characteristics of each region. Students will know characteristics of various cultures and be able to describe the cultures in the settings of Cinderella stories from around the world. Students will know literary elements of a fairy tale and be able to analyze Cinderella stories from around the world. Students will be able to create various forms of writing demonstrating their knowledge of the world. (See Figures 10.1 and 10.2; see pg. 95 for Fig. 10.2.)

Brain Target 4: Declarative and Procedural Knowledge

Activities:

1. Brainstorm with class: What makes a good fairy tale?
2. Think-pair-share: Why do we use writing?

Continents, Oceans, and Landforms Activities:

1. Sing continent and ocean songs.
2. Cut and paste continents and oceans onto a blank world map.

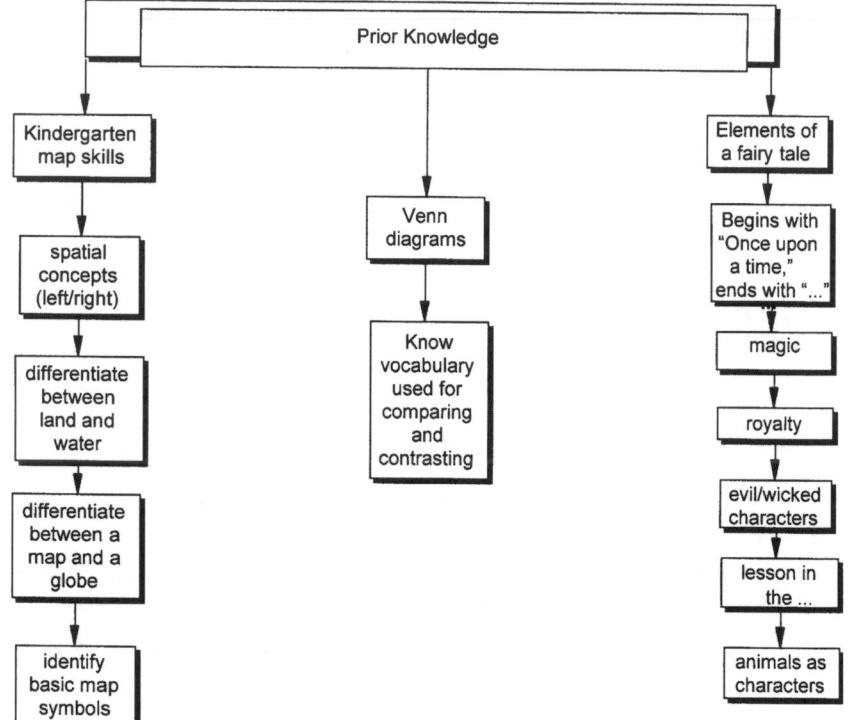

Figure 10.1. *Big-picture activity.*

3. Create a book of geographic landforms with definitions and pictures.
4. Practice reciting and writing personal address.

Map Elements Activities:

1. Recite definition of equator and draw it on a world map.
2. Sing cardinal direction song with associated dance movements.
3. Cooperative groups present definition of equator using classroom map.
4. Learn mnemonic device for cardinal directions.
5. Read a story about the poles. Discuss and chart characteristics of each.
6. Create a "world pumpkin globe" using cutouts of continents, the equator, and poles. Observe teacher cutting the pumpkin in half.

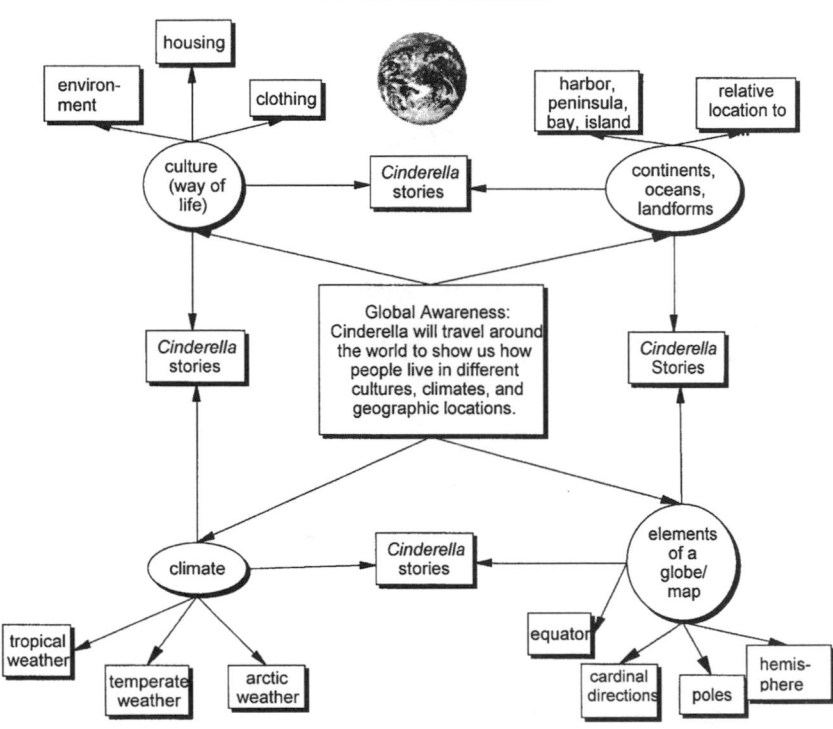

Figure 10.2. Cinderella *big-picture activity.*

Discuss which continents are located entirely in one hemisphere and which are in both.

Climate Activities:

1. Glue cutout weather symbols onto a world map in the appropriate geographic region.
2. View and discuss pictures of various climates. Chart characteristics on board.
3. Create appropriate movement for each climate while moving around the world from equator to poles and back.

Culture Activities:

1. Brainstorm wants and needs of life in our culture.
2. Categorize each into environment, housing, clothing.

Cinderella Stories Activities:

1. Read Perrault's *Cinderella* and identify elements of a fairy tale and setting.
2. Retell the traditional tale of Cinderella.

Writing Activities:

1. Complete postcard template using details appropriate to the setting of Cinderella in Perrault's version.
2. Complete Elements of a Fairy Tale chart.

Brain Target 5: Extension and Application of Knowledge

Continents, Oceans, and Landforms Activities:

1. Create movements for each continent and ocean. Movements will accompany songs.
2. Travel around the world using a floor map. Encourage students to use their movements throughout travel.
3. Review continents, oceans, and landforms by identifying them on a beach ball globe.
4. Create a passport for each student with personal information including country, address, and telephone number. (This passport will be used throughout the unit as we travel around the world.)
5. Have students use stacking cups to provide concrete representation of their position in the world. The largest cup represents the world; decreasing sizes stand for the continent, country, state, city, and neighborhood.

Map Elements Activities:

1. Draw and identify the equator on a variety of spherical fruits.
2. Complete a model compass rose, a visual display of the cardinal directions, and have students create a unique design for their own compass rose.

3. Participate in a scavenger hunt in which the clues use cardinal directions.
4. Complete a Venn diagram comparing the locations, culture, and climate of two of the countries discussed in the unit.
5. Play the hemisphere spinner game.

Climate Activities:

1. Create a travel poster for each of the climates discussed, inviting people to visit.
2. Create a song about world climates.

Culture and Writing Activities:

1. After "flying" to specific continents, read versions of Cinderella story related to that continent (see Figure 10.3).

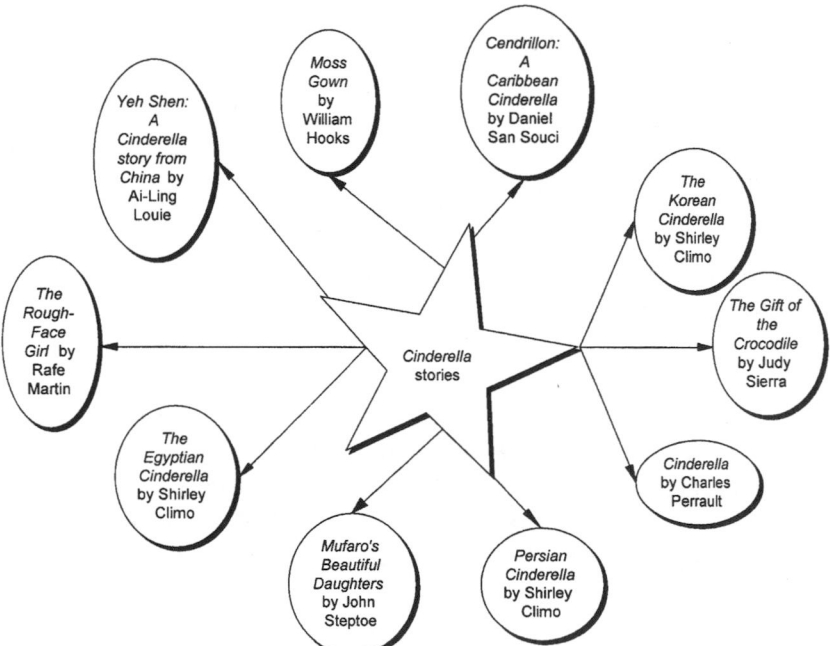

Figure 10.3.   *Versions of* Cinderella *from different continents.*

2. For each story, discuss culture in which that story takes place, complete passport, postcard, and Venn diagram comparing it to the traditional Cinderella story.
3. Chart elements of a fairy tale.
4. Other suggested activities: Sequence plot and draw self as Cinderella before and after magical transformation. Solicit reader-writer responses to a variety of questions (e.g., "How is magic used in the fairy tale *Yen-Shen*?").

Real-World Activities:

1. Play the "Where in the World Is Cinderella?" game. Use student-created clues to identify Cinderella's location. Clues should use geographic and cultural terminology.
2. Create symbols representative of each continent to be used in students' passports.
3. Draw pictures representative of cultures to be used on the front of the postcards.
4. Create a travel brochure advertising the culture and climate of students' favorite continent.
5. Write a Cinderella story from Antarctica or Australia. Include information regarding climate, culture, and elements of a fairy tale.
6. Read the poem "Snowman" by Shel Silverstein. Answer in cooperative groups the question, "Where in the world can you find a snowman in July?"

Brain Target 6: Evaluating Learning

1. On a blank world map, students draw and label the equator, poles, and cardinal directions and color-code the continents by hemispheric location.
2. Students match climate symbols and characteristics to appropriate geographic regions.
3. Teacher assesses the Cinderella story using a rubric.

Materials: blank world map handout, world map and cutouts, continent and ocean song, globe and inflatable globe, stacking cups, teacher-made passports, "Me on the Map" and other supporting literature, floor or carpet map, cardinal direction song and mnemonic device, classroom-size map, spinner game, pumpkin and other fruit, weather symbols, pictures of various climates, Cinderella stories, postcard templates, Venn diagram master copy, Elements of a Fairy Tale chart, art supplies, rubrics.

LEONARDO'S NOTEBOOK

Teacher: Susan Rome

This integrated unit uses the work of Leonardo da Vinci to teach scientific inquiry to 9th-grade students. It could be modified and adapted for learners from the 3rd grade to the 12th. Italian Renaissance ideals and history provide the backdrop for a unit that includes technology (papermaking, the printing press, Leonardo's inventions, and original designs), social studies (Italian history and geography), language arts (reading for understanding and performing tasks and writing to inform and for personal expression), and art (painting and drawing). Through debriefing discussions at the close of each day's lesson, I found that students became intrigued by the life of Leonardo da Vinci and wanted to learn more about him. They also demonstrated a new way of looking at everyday objects. I overheard students discussing how telescopes and microscopes were invented! Because of the many components to the unit, accommodations can be made to shorten the length of time it takes to complete. For example, you could spend just one day on paper-making. The unit is ideal for exceptional learners; every member of your class has an opportunity to learn and feel successful!

BRAIN-TARGETED LEARNING UNIT: ART AND SCIENCE

Title: Leonardo's Notebooks
Grade Level: 9
Time Frame: 3–4 weeks
Social Studies Standards: Relate cultural and artistic changes from the Middle Ages to the Renaissance. Demonstrate ability to relate events on a timeline. Demonstrate ability to sketch a map. Demonstrate an understanding of how the Renaissance still impacts life today—politically, socially, artistically, and technologically.

Writing Standards: Demonstrate understanding of metaphor by creating metaphorical poems in the style of Leonardo's scientific metaphors. Demonstrate ability to write hypotheses in a science journal. Demonstrate ability to write an essay summarizing and extending knowledge.

Reading Standards: Demonstrate ability to read primary and secondary source documents for global understanding. Demonstrate ability to read instructions for a complex multistep process.

Science Standards: Develop hypotheses, sketch simple machines, create sketches for original machines, demonstrate understanding of reversible print.

Art Standards: Demonstrate ability to sketch original works and existing works, make paper, and bind a journal. Demonstrate ability to discuss importance of certain works of art and discuss the life and work of Leonardo da Vinci.

Math Standards: Geometry. Demonstrate ability to use exact measurements to design and apply geometric shapes to sketches of machines based on Leonardo's inventions.

Brain Target 1: Emotional Connection

Activities:

1. Make students feel comfortable about their understanding of the difference between art and science.
2. Tell students about Leonardo's life as a person with "differences" (left-handed, single-parent family, outcast).
3. Accommodate students with learning differences by utilizing multiple intelligences.
4. Integrate hands-on, arts-integrated activities to communicate content and assess learning.

Brain Target 2: Physical Environment

Activities:

1. Display Leonardo's sketches, prints of paintings, and Leonardo's self-portrait around the room, as well as pictures of simple machines and Gutenberg's printing press.

2. Make a wall chart that shows the steps for making paper.
3. Post a map of Italy; use basic Italian vocabulary in lessons as signals to begin or end activities.
4. Display student work.
5. Play Renaissance music at the beginning of class and while students are working individually.
6. Move desks into clusters of four to eight.

Brain Target 3: Big-Picture Activity

Learning Goals: Students will demonstrate understanding of the integration of art and science through an examination of the life and work of Leonardo da Vinci. Students will demonstrate ability to create machines and hypothesize their effectiveness.

Activities:
1. Students review the concept map demonstrating major themes and components of the unit (Figure 10.4). In think-pair-share dyads, they brainstorm what they know about each concept on the web. Each group offers ideas to the class. As they respond, the teacher adds their ideas to the concept map.
2. Students work together as a class to come up with definitions of "art" and "science," which the teacher records. After working collaboratively to develop definitions, two students are asked to look up dictionary definitions.
3. Each student completes a KWL chart indicating what they already know about the unit's art and science concepts and what skills and concepts they anticipate learning during the unit.

Brain Target 4: Declarative and Procedural Knowledge

Learning Goal: Students will acquire background knowledge about the Renaissance and be able to compare it to life in the Middle Ages and life today.

Activities:
1. Read secondary source material and view and interpret images and maps to acquire knowledge about the Renaissance in general and Leonardo da Vinci in particular.

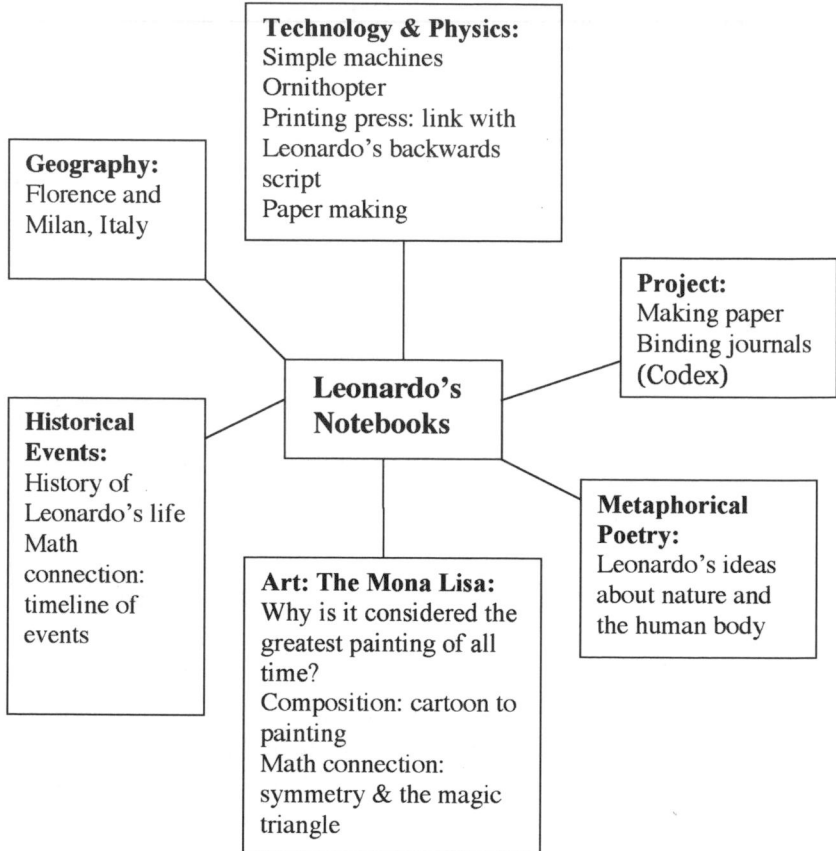

Figure 10.4. Concept map.

2. Plot important dates on a timeline.
3. Sketch a map of Renaissance Italy.
4. Relate cultural and artistic changes from the Middle Ages to the Renaissance, using a T-chart to compare cultures.
5. Use an advanced graphic organizer to demonstrate an understanding of how the Renaissance still impacts life today—politically (e.g., Ducal system vs. democracy), socially (e.g., the guild system vs. the class system), artistically (patrons and artists), and technologically (Gutenberg's press vs. desktop publishing).

Learning Goal: Students will create codices (journals) for their scientific and artistic explorations and sketch certain machines, such as levers, pulleys, screws, and the reversible print press.

Activities:
1. Students read instructions for the multistep process of making paper and a codex.
2. Using reproductions from Leonardo's codices, students hypothesize the use of his inventions.
3. As an introduction to reversible print, students will examine Leonardo's backward left-handed script and hypothesize three reasons why he might have written that way.
4. Looking at existing drawings, students sketch versions of the machines listed above in their journals.
5. In their journals, students write their hypotheses for the use of the machines.

Brain Target 5: Extension and Application of Knowledge

Learning Goal: After identifying a real-life practical problem, students will be able to design a machine.

Activities:
1. In small groups, students discuss practical problems they have, such as disliking ironing clothes for school. They choose one problem to solve.
2. After identifying a common problem for each group, individuals sketch a machine to solve the problem.
3. Each student develops a scientific hypothesis for the inventions.

Learning Goal: Students will be able to identify Leonardo's metaphors for the human body and the natural world.

Activities:
1. Students write metaphorical poems in the style of Leonardo's scientific metaphors.
2. They illustrate their poems in codices.
3. They share poetry by reading aloud.

Learning Goal: Students will be able to sketch a copy of the Mona Lisa and discuss the painting critically.

Activities:

1. Students sketch and paint an existing work, using concepts of composition, symmetry, color theory, and background and foreground.
2. Students discuss the importance of Renaissance art.

Learning Goal: Students will be able to write an essay on Leonardo's work and its relevance today.

Activity: Write a five-paragraph essay on how the work of Leonardo da Vinci is relevant today, concluding with an analysis of "The Renaissance Man (or Woman) of the 21st Century."

Brain Target 6: Evaluating Learning

1. Respond to questions regarding facts, images, and geography of the Renaissance in general and Leonardo da Vinci in particular.
2. Check maps and timelines for accuracy.
3. Review T-chart and use assessment to review and reteach Middle Ages.
4. Use a rubric to evaluate advanced graphic organizer.
5. Determine if all students were able to follow instructions for making paper and journal.
6. Have students self-assess if their hypotheses regarding Leonardo's inventions were correct.
7. Use a rubric to evaluate hypotheses.
8. Use a rubric to evaluate sketches of screws, pulleys, levers, and printing press to determine if all working parts are labeled.
9. Use a rubric to evaluate sketches and hypotheses of original inventions.
10. Check poems for their use of metaphor.
11. Use a rubric to evaluate the presence of components in paintings.
12. Provide an anchor paper for students to peer-edit essays. Let students write multiple drafts. Use a rubric for final drafts.

13. Have students self-evaluate by updating their KWL charts.
14. Administer end-of-unit test. Essay may be part of the test.

Materials: world history textbook and supplementary materials, including Leonardo's *Codex Leicester,* Renaissance and medieval art history books, Internet-connected computers, transparencies of Leonardo's work, photos of northern Italy, models or photos of simple machines, illustration showing how printing press works, overhead projector, paper-making materials or paper to make 8-page journals, mirrors (for decoding backwards writing), CD player and Renaissance CDs, pencils, white paper, tempera paints, brushes, cups for water, rulers and compasses.

SALAD SCIENCE

Teacher: Linda Bluth

It is my experience that children will readily embrace science when it is presented in a way that engages all their senses, as opposed to just reading from text or looking at pictures. Students have fun munching a piece of cucumber and trying to figure out why it is a fruit. By directly experiencing the way a plant changes throughout its life cycle, students are able to integrate how plants become the foods they eat. They might even become interested in trying some new foods.

BRAIN-TARGETED LEARNING UNIT: SCIENCE

Title: Salad Science
Grade Level: 3
Time Frame: 2–3 weeks
Science Standard: Demonstrate the ability to use scientific skills and processes to explain the dynamic nature of living things, their interactions, and the results from the interactions that occur over time.
Math Standard: Demonstrate the ability to collect, organize, display, and interpret data.
Writing Standard: Demonstrate the ability to write to inform by developing and organizing facts to convey information.

Brain Target 1: Emotional Connection

Activities:

1. Connect students to the concept that all living things have special body parts that allow them to do certain things by exploring parts of leaves and their functions. Ask them to pick up their pencil with an elbow. Lead them to conclude that our hands are designed to grab and how this is so. Relate this to the leaf parts.
2. Include visual arts by having students make rubbings of leaves to be displayed. As they are making their rubbings, they will write down any observations or questions.
3. Include music by having students make up and sing songs about plants.
4. At the beginning of each lesson ask students to either state something they have learned or ask a question related to our study.
5. Allow students to evaluate their own cognitive learning on a KWL chart.

Brain Target 2: Physical Environment

Activities:

1. Display pictures of many kinds of plants.
2. Create a bulletin board showing the life cycle of a pumpkin.
3. Display pictures of the specialized parts of plants and cover up the text that the students will be asked to write later on.
4. Create a science table to display growing plants in various stages of development.
5. Create a reading corner to display plant books with colorful pictures and simple text.
6. Display students' rubbings and drawings on classroom clothesline.
7. Arrange desks in clusters for cooperative activities.
8. Have students keep all materials generated through the unit in a science journal folder.

Brain Target 3: Big-Picture Activity

Learning Goals: Students will demonstrate knowledge of the develop-ment of a plant from a seed and the specialized function of the six main body parts of a plant.

Activities:
1. Give students a blank concept map, "Life Cycle of a Flowering Plant," and ask what *cycle* means and why a plant's life is dis-played as a circle. After developing the meaning for *germinate* and *pollinate,* guide students in completing the map.
2. Ask students to highlight the six main plant parts: seed, root, stem, leaf, flower, and fruit. Say to students, "Remember the les-son learned from trying to pick up your pencil with your elbow? We will be learning the special job of each of these plant parts." Give students a partially completed concept map, "Flowering Plants," and have them complete the map by adding the function of each part as they now perceive it. They may discuss this with a partner. At the end of the unit we will eat various salad foods as we identify the part of the plant being nibbled.

Brain Target 4: Declarative and Procedural Knowledge

Learning Goals: Students will know the six main parts of a flowering plant and be able to identify its specialized function. Students will be able to measure the growth of a seedling and record and graph this data.

Activities:
1. After asking students what they know and what they'd like to know about seeds, give each one a soaked lima bean seed and a hand lens. They open the seed and draw and label the parts. To-gether develop the purpose of a seed and how all seeds are alike. Partners check each other's work. Then plant some seeds in clear cups so students can see the roots as they grow. They will draw these and speculate on the function of roots.
2. Start some bean plants ahead of time so that each group of stu-dents can observe, write about, and measure the growth of its

plant. Collect measurement data daily and display it in a bar graph.

3. Students read "The Seedling" by Paul L. Dunbar as a way to review the stages of plant growth. They also complete a grid comparing themselves to a seedling: what kind of work we do, what we need, and what we will become.

4. Students observe celery stalks under three different conditions: in water, in no water, in water colored with food dye. They then draw their observations and write about the job of a stem. Develop this concept as a group.

5. Tell students that the job of a flower is to make new seeds so the plant can reproduce itself. Give them a real flower to observe, draw, and figure out how this happens. Together develop the process and label the parts of a flower.

6. Show students an apple and a green pepper and tell them they are two examples of fruit. Cut both open and ask how they are alike (they both contain seeds). Show a picture of an apple tree in bloom. Students dialogue with partner to figure out how flowers become apples. Share ideas and affirm correct details of the process. Give each student an edamame (soybean) and ask them to figure out why this is a fruit. Open it up and eat the peas (seeds).

Brain Target 5: Extension and Application of Knowledge

Learning Goal: Students will know the plant part of a given food and be able to write a brief article demonstrating their understanding.

Activity: Present students with a salad bar from which they may choose several items. They must observe and draw the foods and decide which part of the plant they come from and why. Then ask them to pick one of the items and write an illustrated article for a child's botany book.

Brain Target 6: Evaluating Learning

1. Have partners check each other's work using a class-generated rubric.
2. Use a rubric to evaluate the graphs.

3. Have students share their science journal entry with their group and receive feedback.
4. Use an anchor paper to allow students to self-grade and correct descriptions.
5. Have students self-evaluate the productiveness of their conversation.
6. Use science/writing checklist to evaluate botany article.
7. Provide ongoing self-evaluation by using KWL chart.
8. Administer end-of-unit test.

Materials: seeds and soil for planting; plants for eating: edamames, lettuce, tomato, cucumber, pear, kiwi, broccoli, carrot, celery, peanuts in shells; one lima bean and hand lens per student; one bean plant just beginning to emerge for each group; "The Seedling" by Paul L. Dunbar; celery stalks, apples and green peppers; one flower per student; two concept maps per student; one science journal folder per student; one template for botany book article/illustration per student.

JULIUS CAESAR TODAY

Teacher: Laurie Frank

I love doing this unit with my students. Besides giving me the chance to teach them about Shakespeare's writing, the unit also opens up all kinds of possibilities for creative endeavor by incorporating theater activities into the lessons. Such activities motivate students to use and interpret language in a spoken context and create a positive, supportive classroom atmosphere for both low- and high-achieving students. In addition, Shakespeare's plays, *Julius Caesar* especially, relate beautifully to contemporary themes, affording meaningful opportunities for extending learning and developing higher thinking skills.

BRAIN-TARGETED LEARNING UNIT: LANGUAGE ARTS

Title: Julius Caesar Today
Grade Level: 7
Time Frame: 1–2 weeks

Writing Standard: Demonstrate the ability to write to express personal ideas and to inform.

Reading Standard: Demonstrate the ability to read a variety of texts for global understanding and interpreting details.

Listening Standard: Demonstrate the ability to participate using an active listening process.

Brain Target 1: Emotional Connection

Activities:

1. Connect students to the concept of writing about a time period and place they have never experienced. Ask students to write an opening paragraph of a short story with a setting given to them by the teacher. The students research the time and place in order to create a believable setting for their story.
2. Include lessons on the research project along with ample time for using the library.
3. Integrate theater activities as part of the lessons.
4. Offer assistance to students with special needs; use multiple modalities to demonstrate learning.
5. Allow students to evaluate their own cognitive and social learning on a KWL chart.

Brain Target 2: Physical Environment

Activities:

1. Plan the following classroom configurations to be used during the unit: Cooperative groups of six; a theater-style setup with desks and chairs arranged in a semi-circle around a central performing area; a full circle of chairs.
2. Display pictures of Shakespeare, Julius Caesar, ancient Rome, and Shakespeare's England.
3. Display student products.

Brain Target 3: Big-Picture Activity

Learning Goal: Students will demonstrate understanding of the differences between Shakespeare's England and ancient Rome.

Activities:

1. Students complete two KWL charts indicating what they already know about Shakespeare's England and ancient Rome and what they want to learn during the unit.
2. Divide students into groups to research different aspects of the two historical periods. Groups can be arranged according to the following topics: clothes, food, entertainment, government, family life, architecture.
3. Each group shares the results of its research with other groups using a jigsaw format.
4. Each student completes a Venn diagram comparing and contrasting the two different time periods and places.

Brain Target 4: Declarative and Procedural Knowledge

Learning Goal: Students will know the arguments for and against the assassination of Julius Caesar and be able to present oral and written statements defending one of the two positions.

Activities:
1. Divide students into groups of six and ask each group to complete a T-chart identifying the main arguments in favor of and opposed to the assassination of Caesar.
2. Discuss with the class all topics pertinent to the brainstorming session.
3. Organize a circle debate in which students assume roles as citizens of Rome and present arguments for or against the assassination of Julius Caesar. Students sit in a circle; one student begins the debate with a statement taking a pro or con position; the next person says "I agree" or "I disagree" and gives a reason; the debate continues until all students have participated.
4. Students use information from their T-charts and the debate to complete a writing prompt based on their opinions of Julius Caesar's assassination. Sample prompt: Suppose you are a Roman citizen writing a letter to your brother, a Roman soldier in Gaul. Inform your brother about Caesar's assassination and give your opinion as to whether or not it was a good thing. Be sure

to support your opinions using information discussed during the debate.

Brain Target 5: Extension and Application of Knowledge

Learning Goal: Students will know people, places, and events from Julius Caesar and be able to develop and interpret characterizations based on their knowledge.

Activities:
1. Divide students into groups and assign each group a brief scene from *Julius Caesar.* The students use class time to create a realistic interpretation of the scene; they may use costumes and props. A few mini-lessons on acting may be necessary to help students gain a better understanding of Shakespearean theater.
2. Students use the theater-style classroom configuration to present and discuss each of the scenes presented.

Brain Target 6: Evaluating Learning

1. Review KWL chart; determine degree of students' prior knowledge.
2. Use a scoring tool to evaluate Venn diagram.
3. Use a participation checklist to evaluate student performance during circle debate.
4. Use rubric to evaluate student letter to Roman soldier.
5. Have students create a rubric to be used to evaluate their presentations.

Materials: Julius Caesar play, reference books, "Inspiration for Kids" software, T-charts, KWL charts, Venn diagrams, rubrics.

ASUNTOS DOMESTICOS (DOMESTIC ISSUES)

Teacher: Elayne Melanson

Motivating high school students to learn Spanish to a level of proficiency is a challenge when they perceive it as a "foreign" language that requires travel to render it useful. It is also a challenge to motivate students based on the premise that it may be useful to them in their careers. And we all know how much teenagers are interested in the home and domestic chores! This unit, entitled Domestic Issues, will make learning grammar and vocabulary meaningful by enabling students to apply their Spanish language skills to a real-life, purposeful experience.

BRAIN-TARGETED LEARNING UNIT: FOREIGN LANGUAGE

Title: Asuntos Domesticos (Domestic Issues)
Grade Level: high school Spanish level III
Time Frame: 3 weeks (one week each of culture, thematic vocabulary and grammar, culminating activity and assessment)
Foreign Language National Standard(s):
Goal 1: Communicate in Languages Other Than English: Students will engage in conversations, provide and obtain information, express feelings and emotions, and exchange opinions. Students will understand and interpret written and spoken language on a variety of topics. Students will present information, concepts, and ideas to an audience of listeners or readers on a variety of topics.
Goal 2: Gain Knowledge and Understanding of Other Cultures: Students will demonstrate an understanding of the relationship between the practices and perspective of the culture studied.
Goal 3: Connect with Other Disciplines and Acquire Information: Students will reinforce and further their knowledge of other disciplines through the foreign language. Students will acquire information and recognize the distinctive viewpoints that are available only through the foreign language and its culture.
Goal 4: Develop Insight into the Nature of Language and Culture: Students will demonstrate understanding of the nature of language through comparisons of the language studied and their own. Students will demonstrate understanding of the concept of culture through comparisons of the cultures studied and their own.
Goal 5: Participate in Multilingual Communities at Home and Around the World: Students will use the language both within and beyond the school setting.

Brain Target 1: Emotional Environment

Activities:

1. Connect students to the concept of Spanish language learning as a "domestic" issue through an awareness and appreciation of the Hispanic population in their own country and local community.
2. Have students experience through a role-play how it feels to be a non-English-speaking worker in the U.S.
3. Connect students through a simulated interview to the experience of a non-English-speaking Hispanic in the United States workforce.
4. Connect students to the concepts of learning thematic vocabulary about domestic tasks and the imperative mood in Spanish grammar by tutoring native Spanish speakers who are preparing to work in the U.S.

Brain Target 2: Physical Environment

Activities:

1. Create displays of photographs and posters depicting people and places in the U.S. and in the immediate community reflecting the Hispanic presence.
2. Read and display U.S. documents originally written in Spanish.
3. Play current musical selections that reflect the Hispanic influence on music in the U.S.
4. Show video clips related to the Hispanic presence in the U.S.
5. Have the students prepare bulletin board of selected articles from national and local newspapers related to Hispanic issues in the U.S.
6. Display maps of the world, the U.S., and the local community, to be marked to indicate where Spanish is spoken as a first or second language.
7. Arrange desks for cooperative group activities, pair work, and debate, as appropriate.
8. Display student products.

Brain Target 3: Big-Picture Activity

Learning Goal: Students will demonstrate an awareness of the Hispanic presence in their own country and community. Students will demonstrate the ability to understand in the affirmative and negative formal imperative mood spoken and written Spanish instructions pertaining to domestic chores. Students will demonstrate the ability to use the affirmative and negative formal imperative mood and appropriate vocabulary to communicate verbal and written instructions related to domestic chores.

Culture Activities:
1. Students think-pair-share to give possible explanations for the title of the unit, *Asuntos Domesticos.*
2. Students brainstorm in groups and share with the class how the concept of domestic chores can be related to other domestic issues within a country.
3. Students participate in an activity called "Domestic or Foreign" to assess their own prior knowledge of the Hispanic presence in the U.S. By clapping under their desks (to avoid possible embarrassment at being incorrect) in response to teacher-selected audiovisuals, such as pictures, music, video clips, and artifacts, students indicate by one clap if they believe the item represents something found in the U.S. (domestic) rather than something foreign (outside the U.S.). After each item is shown and the response is given, the teacher indicates whether the item is domestic or foreign. (Select items that students might be inclined to think are foreign but are actually domestic, such as a Spanish sign in a U.S. town that says, "English is spoken here.")
4. Students volunteer to put marks on classroom maps of the world, the U.S., and their local community. The marks indicate places where Spanish is spoken as a first or second language. (A red dot indicates first language; a blue dot indicates second language.) Students at their seats mark handout copies of the maps in the same way.
5. Students participate in a true/false survey, which includes facts about the Hispanic workforce, to assess their prior knowledge

concerning the Hispanic population in the U.S. and in their own community. They respond on a worksheet to true/false statements. The number of true and false responses are compared with the correct response. (Use information such as percentage of workforce in the U.S. that is Hispanic, percentage of the Hispanic workforce in the U.S. performing in a domestic occupation, percentage of Hispanic workers in the U.S. who do not speak English.)

6. Students participate in a four-corners activity to determine their prior experience with the Hispanic presence in the U.S. The teacher marks each corner of the room A, B, C, or D, then asks a series of questions, and students move to the corner if their answer is yes. Corner A: Do you know someone who speaks Spanish outside the classroom? Where? At home? At work? On a trip? Corner B: Do you know someone who is bilingual? Spanish first language, English second? Who? From what country? Is the person a citizen of the U.S.? Is the person visiting? What does the person do for a living? Corner C: How many of you know someone who lives in the U.S. but can only speak Spanish? Who? Is the person working here? How does this person communicate with others? Through an interpreter? Why did that person come to live in the U.S.? Corner D: How many of you have encountered Spanish speakers in your own community? Where? In school? In a restaurant?

7. Students participate in a debate. The teacher divides the room into two sections facing each other. Students write their names on index cards. They listen to a statement and write "agree" or "disagree" on the card. The teacher collects the cards and assigns the debate teams. (This way students will not choose a side based on their friends or the most popular response.) Students work cooperatively to prepare debate statements to justify their opinions and follow-up questions. Example of statement: "Hispanics living in the U.S. should be required to speak English in order to work here."

8. Students develop an awareness of how it feels to be a nonnative speaker in the workforce by participating in a TPR (Total Physical Response) activity led by the teacher. The teacher provides props, such as tools used for domestic occupations and verbally gives each student a task using the new thematic vocabulary and

the new concept of the imperative. ("Sweep the floor with a broom today," or "Make all the beds with the clean sheets.") The activity is followed up with a discussion of how the students felt during the experience and how they think a Spanish speaker working in the U.S. without English skills might feel in that same situation.

Vocabulary Activities: Students individually receive a list of thematic vocabulary words and phrases in English with blank lines following. As they have some prior knowledge of basic vocabulary about the home, they use black ink to fill in what they already know. They then move into cooperative groups and share answers. Any words they did not know on their own, they fill in with green ink. When all groups have finished, the entire class reviews the list with the teacher for accuracy, correcting incorrect responses and filling in blank ones with red ink. Any words written in green or red are ones they don't know.

Grammar Activities: Students fill out a KWL chart. Under "What I Know," they fill out the first-person-singular present tense of verbs that will be used in the unit. This is preparation for learning what they need to know about forming imperatives. (In Spanish, the formal imperative is based on the first-person-singular form of the verb in the present tense.) They divide the second column into columns for affirmative singular command, negative singular command, affirmative plural command, and negative plural command. These columns remain blank. The last column, designated for what they have learned, is arranged the same way as the second column. Following instruction on the imperative mood, students complete the third column to show what they have learned.

Brain Target 4: Declarative and Procedural Knowledge

Learning Goal 1: Students will become aware of Hispanic issues in the U.S. and in their own communities.

Activity: Students prepare a bulletin board of articles from national and local newspapers and magazines related to Hispanic issues in the U.S.

Before putting their articles on the bulletin board, each student must tell the class the main idea of the article.

Learning Goal 2: Students will know vocabulary from English to Spanish and from Spanish to English to communicate about domestic tasks.

Activities:
1. Students play the "Go Fish" card game in groups of four. They use their vocabulary lists to select vocabulary they did not know, selecting from the list of words written in green or red. They write the words on index cards (Spanish on one card, English on the other). They shuffle the group's cards together and play "Go Fish," which involves matching English and Spanish pairs of words or expressions.
2. Students play "Password" in groups. One student in the group has a list of vocabulary words and expressions. This person must try to get the others in the group to say the word without speaking English, without using gestures, and without using any word or expression on their list. Each student in the group gets a list and proceeds in this manner.

Learning Goal 3: Students will know how to form the formal affirmative and negative commands in the singular and plural.

Activity: Students use the KWL list they completed. The teacher writes the imperative form of some of those verbs on the board. Students brainstorm to come up with the pattern for forming imperatives and complete the rest of the chart based on the pattern.

Brain Target 5: Extension and Application of Knowledge

Activities:

1. Using the imperative and thematic vocabulary, students work in groups to produce written bilingual instructions for the tasks to be done for a domestic occupation (i.e., hotel domestic worker, construction laborer).

2. In groups of three, students role-play to integrate and apply knowledge of the grammar and vocabulary learned. One student assumes the role of employer and the other two the roles of employees in a domestic occupational setting. (They will switch roles so that each person gets to be the employer once.) The employer gives verbal commands in the singular and plural, negative and affirmative. The employee(s) respond appropriately by performing the action.

3. As a home assignment, students prepare five questions in Spanish to interview a native speaker about his or her experience working in the U.S. without English fluency. The teacher corrects the assignment prior to the visit and marks one question on each student's paper to be asked on the day of the interview. The teacher provides a written list of the questions to be asked by the students before the interview. During the interview, students take notes based on the speaker's response to each question. The students use their notes as a guideline to write reflective essays on their feelings about what was learned.

4. This culminating activity is based on the concept that, after a month, we learn and remember 92% of what we teach others, 14% of what we hear, 22% of what we see, 30% of what we watch others do, 42% from sensory redundancy, 72% of events linked to remembered or imagined life experiences, and 83% from a first-time or demanding action that applies the new learning. Students participate in an authentic day of service, which is arranged between the teacher and an organization in the community that serves the needs of Hispanics. Spanish speakers in need of English tutoring to prepare for a domestic occupation are paired with students in the class. Students apply vocabulary and grammar skills to help teach native Spanish speakers essential on-the-job English words and phrases, relative to domestic occupations. The service day arrangements could be made by having the students visit the community organization for the day or by having the organization bring those who need such tutoring to the class on a given day. Profiles of the individual's needs are provided to each student prior to the tutoring session. (The school administration would need to approve this day as a field trip experience.)

Brain Target 6: Evaluation of Learning

Cultural Awareness Assessment: Based on the student's newly acquired cultural awareness, he or she writes an essay in answer to the question: Is it an advantage to be bilingual (Spanish/English) in the United States? Use rubrics for assessment.

Listening and Speaking Assessment: The students act as interpreters to assess their speaking and listening skills. A student role-plays as an English interpreter by repeating in English what the teacher says in Spanish. A student role-plays as a Spanish interpreter by repeating in Spanish what the teacher says in English. Use rubrics for assessment.

Reading and Writing Assessment: Students act as translators, as they did as interpreters. They read a set of Spanish domestic-job-related instructions and write them in English. They also read a set of domestic-job-related instructions in English and write them in Spanish. Use rubrics for assessment.

Materials: classroom size maps of world, U.S., local community; handout of maps; blue and red dots (or pushpins); photographs, artifacts, documents, video clips, musical selections related to Hispanic presence in the U.S.; CD player; TV/VCR or DVD player; true/false cultural worksheet; red, black, and green pens; KWL chart; vocabulary list handout; index cards; password lists; supplies to prepare bulletin board; items used to perform domestic tasks, i.e., broom, mop, rag, trash can, etc.; chalkboard, dry-erase board, or overhead projector; signs A, B, C, D to mark four corners of the room.

CHAPTER 11

School Improvement Planning

Whether labeled as "high-performing" or "failing," all schools can improve. Refining an effective school or overhauling one that is troubled begins by inspecting the school's foundation. That is, the school improvement process must consider how well a school translates its vision and mission into practice: Does the school actually do what it says it does? If a school claims, for example, that teachers "provide challenging learning experiences to help each child reach his or her full potential," school stakeholders should know if this statement is true in each classroom for every child.

The process of evaluating the degree to which a school implements its vision and mission, determines its effectiveness, and plans for improvement is often complex and sometimes cumbersome. It begins with diagnosing school performance on indicators such as student achievement, school climate, parent and community involvement, faculty and staff retention rates, student and faculty attendance, high school completion rates, compliance with federal laws for educating students with disabilities, and so forth.

The next stages of school improvement planning typically involve identifying and prioritizing goals for improvement, establishing activities and measurable indicators for achieving those goals, and evaluating the degree to which goals have been met. While the actual format of school improvement plans may vary among states, school districts, and even among schools within a district, the process of school improvement planning usually includes the essential elements of diagnosing, goal-setting, action-planning, and evaluating.

A school improvement plan based on brain-targeted teaching connects these elements to each of the six brain targets. To begin a process of diagnosis compatible with what we have learned about brain research, this chapter provides school-effectiveness indicators for each brain target. Administrators and school improvement teams could evaluate their schools relative to these indicators and select one or more to incorporate into a school improvement plan. The last section of this chapter provides a sample school improvement plan that demonstrates how each brain target indicator can be developed into a plan of action for school reform.

The requirements of the Elementary and Secondary Education Act "No Child Left Behind" have brought a new level of accountability for student achievement to our nation's schools. Many educators fear that this accountability will drive schools to focus instructional time on preparing students for high-stakes standardized testing through rote learning activities. It is perhaps more critical now than ever before that educators advocate for learning experiences that apply research from the fields of neurology and cognitive sciences that informs us about how the brain thinks and learns.

We are about to embark upon an exciting yet challenging time for educators—one that will hold us accountable for our students' achievement on standardized tests but also demand that we prepare them for high levels of thinking so they can skillfully and creatively address the problems of the new century. As schools face these challenges, many new educators are entering the teaching ranks. Severe teacher shortages in some parts of the country will require school districts to hire teachers without certification or practice teaching experience. We believe that the brain-targeted teaching model will assist new educators and inspire veteran teachers in the planning and implementation of exciting lessons, units, and experiences that result in active, meaningful learning for all children.

SCHOOL-EFFECTIVENESS INDICATORS

Brain-Target 1: Emotional Climate for Learning

- A climate of mutual respect encompasses all members of the school community, including students, teachers, administrators, and parents.

- Students trust and feel nurtured by adults in the classroom and in every aspect of school life, including extracurricular activities, counseling activities, and sports activities.
- Multiculturalism is recognized and celebrated.
- Students display their talents through a wide array of activities incorporating the use of multiple intelligences.
- Learning differences are skillfully accommodated within the classroom setting.
- Parents support learning goals through volunteer activities.
- Teachers and administrators recognize parents' role in school improvement and reform.
- Staff members are empowered to take risks without negative consequences.
- Students with social/emotional difficulties are provided with appropriate interventions.

Brain-Target 2: Physical Learning Environment

- The physical plant, including classrooms, cafeteria, and restrooms, is clean and in good repair.
- The school campus, including grounds, playgrounds, and fields, is appropriately maintained.
- The grounds are visually appealing with shrubs, flowers, and art.
- The school building is visually appealing with murals, awards, posters, etc.
- The halls are brightly lit, with as much natural lighting as possible.
- Vertical and horizontal spaces in the school and classrooms are neat and orderly.
- Halls and classroom walls display students' art and written work.
- Multicultural art is included in classroom and school displays.
- Classrooms include natural lighting, appropriate temperature, and acceptable noise levels.

Brain-Target 3: Designing Learning Outcomes

- National and state standards are used in curriculum planning.
- The school develops and uses a multidisciplinary scope and sequence that spirals content and skills through each grade.

- Teachers use concept maps and other visual representations to help students understand key concepts.
- Instructional objectives for each lesson are written in measurable terms, describing what students will know and be able to do as a result of instruction.
- Learning goals and instructional objectives are visibly displayed in classrooms.
- Teachers have scheduled time for collaborative planning within and across grade levels, within content areas, and in interdisciplinary teams.
- Teachers have ongoing professional development, mentoring, and coaching.
- Teachers share learning units in a professional library.

Brain-Target 4: Declarative and Procedural Knowledge

- Reading, mathematics, and writing skill programs reflect the needs of remedial as well as accomplished achievers.
- Teachers use a wide array of activities to reinforce learning objectives.
- Teachers use multiple modalities and multiple intelligences to reinforce learning objectives.
- Schedule allows teachers to give students "think and reflection" time to consolidate learning every 20 minutes.
- Learning activities build on prior knowledge.
- Homework reinforces learning objectives.

Brain-Target 5: Extension, Integration, and Application of Knowledge

- Teachers design activities that extend acquired knowledge to performance-based tasks requiring students to solve problems using real-world settings.
- Visual and performing arts are integrated into learning activities.
- Teachers effectively integrate technology into learning activities to support higher-level thinking and learning.

- Learning is extended through activities that require comparison, classification, inductive and deductive thinking, analyzing perspectives, defending positions.
- Learning is extended through activities that require experimental inquiry, investigation, and invention.

Brain-Target 6: Evaluating Learning

- Teachers post on the board measurable objectives that describe what students will know and be able to do as a result of instruction.
- Objectives are measured during the lesson.
- Teachers use performance-based activities to assess learning outcomes.
- Teachers use rubrics to give students relevant feedback about their performance.
- Evaluation includes both oral and written responses.
- Quizzes and tests allow for both selected and constructed responses.
- Student portfolios are used to demonstrate student learning.
- Teacher portfolios are used to demonstrate student learning.
- Evaluation allows for multiple modalities and multiple intelligences.

BRAIN-TARGETED TEACHING SCHOOL IMPROVEMENT PLAN

Brain Target 1: Setting the Emotional Climate

Brain Target Indicator: Multiculturalism is recognized and celebrated.
School Improvement Goal: Classroom materials and extracurricular activities will include multicultural themes.
Objective 1: Students will gain an understanding of cultural diversity and display their knowledge of various cultures through creative writing, art, and dramatic performances.

Activities:
1. Have each class in the school discuss cultural diversity and choose a culture to study through novels, plays, or other narrative or expository texts.

2. Have each class prepare a book review, skit, play, song, or dance that displays features of their chosen culture.
3. Present a school-wide assembly to display the features of the various cultures investigated by each class.

Evaluation: Students will complete a self-evaluation survey that identifies how their understanding and appreciation of cultural diversity has changed as a result of the activities.
Timeline: First semester
Person Responsible: Master teacher, assistant principal, department chair
Budget: Funds necessary to purchase novels, support visual displays, costumes, etc.
Objective 2: Classroom texts and supplementary materials will reflect cultural diversity.

Activities:
1. Examine classroom texts to determine the degree to which they reflect a diversity of races and cultures.
2. Post classroom visual displays that reflect multiple races and cultures.
3. Include multicultural themes and topics in supplementary teaching materials, such as novels, plays, or expository text.

Evaluation: Teachers and administrators complete a survey using a five-point Likert Scale to determine the degree to which texts, classroom displays, and supplementary materials reflect multicultural themes.
Timeline: Second semester
Person Responsible: Subcommittee of school improvement team
Budget: None

Brain Target 2: Creating the Physical Learning Environment

Brain Target Indicator: The school building is visually appealing with murals, awards, posters, etc.
School Improvement Goal: To improve the appearance of the school through student-created art.

Objective: Artists will work with students to paint murals to provide cheerful, attractive halls, cafeteria, and lavatories.

Activities:
1. Seek out resources among faculty, staff, and parents to donate time to instruct and direct students in the completion of wall murals throughout the school.
2. Seek out resources outside the school community, such as businesses, colleges and universities, and practicing artists, to volunteer time to instruct and direct students in the completion of wall murals throughout the school.

Evaluation: Log of contacts and responses; completion of task
Timeline: First three months of school year
Persons Responsible: School improvement team subcommittee members
Budget: Funds necessary to purchase painting supplies, possible stipend

Brain Target 3: Designing Learning Outcomes

Brain Target Indicator: Teachers use concept maps and other visual representations to help students understand key concepts.
School Improvement Goal: Students will demonstrate global understanding of content through the use of visual representations.
Objective: All teachers will use concept maps to help students understand key ideas and concepts of units of study.

Activities:
1. Determine through needs assessment instruments, surveys, and lesson plans which teachers regularly use concept maps to help students understand big-picture ideas of learning units.
2. Use professional development sessions, individual peer-coaching, and mentoring to train teachers to effectively incorporate concept mapping into instructional planning.
3. Use computer software such as "Inspiration" to help teachers and students construct concept maps.

Evaluation: Examination of teacher and student portfolios, examination of lesson plans, teacher surveys
Timeline: First months of school year
Persons Responsible: Staff development committee, administrators
Budget: Funds necessary to purchase computer software programs

Brain Target 4: Teaching for Declarative and Procedural Knowledge

Brain Target Indicator: Teachers use multiple modalities and multiple intelligences to reinforce learning goals.
School Improvement Goal: Teachers will use a variety of activities that use multiple intelligences to teach and assess learning objectives.
Objective: Teachers will infuse art and music into instructional activities.

Activities:
1. Offer professional development on the use of multiple intelligences; provide books, journal articles, and videos that demonstrate effective integration of art and music into learning tasks.
2. Survey teachers to determine those who currently infuse art and music into instructional activities.
3. Offer "best practices" workshops, where teachers share lesson plans that infuse art and music into instructional activities.
4. Arrange for teachers to observe and coteach with colleagues in arts and music integration lessons.
5. Create a professional reference library for teachers to share books, journal articles, and exemplary arts-integration lesson plans.

Evaluation: Examination of teacher and student portfolios, examination of lesson plans, teacher surveys
Timeline: Second semester of school year
Persons Responsible: Staff development committee, administrators
Budget: Funds necessary to purchase books and other professional development materials

Brain Target 5: Teaching for Extension and Application of Knowledge

Brain Target Indicator: Teachers design activities that extend acquired knowledge to performance-based tasks requiring students to solve problems using real-world settings.

School Improvement Goal: All teachers will extend learning by designing activities that require students to apply knowledge through real-world problem-solving tasks.

Objective: Teachers will design one activity per quarter requiring students to apply learning in performance-based tasks.

Activities:
1. Provide professional development session in which one learning activity within various disciplines (mathematics, language arts, social studies, science) demonstrates real-world application of content in a problem-solving task.
2. Facilitate peer coaching sessions so that a teacher with expertise in designing performance-based activities can assist a novice teacher by helping with initial planning of the lesson, observing its implementation, providing feedback, and suggesting revisions.
3. Collect and include in the professional library resources from the Internet and printed materials that demonstrate performance-based instruction.
4. Facilitate small groups of teachers to develop interdisciplinary brain-targeted teaching units.

Evaluation: Examination of teacher and student portfolios, examination of lesson plans, teacher surveys

Timeline: Entire school year

Persons Responsible: Staff development committee, administrators, department chairs, master teachers

Budget: Funds necessary to purchase books and other professional development materials, stipend for presenters for staff development sessions

Brain Target 6: Evaluating Learning

Brain Target Indicator: Teachers use rubrics to give students relevant feedback about their performance.
School Improvement Goal: All teachers will use rubrics to evaluate writing and performance-based tasks.
Objective: Teachers will design a rubric to assess writing assignments.

Activities:
1. Provide professional development session on the construction and use of scoring rubrics to assess student writing.
2. Invite each teacher to submit to a school-wide resource bank one scoring rubric that they developed for their class.
3. Empower students to design scoring rubrics to demonstrate their understanding of an activity or assignment.

Evaluation: Examination of teacher and student portfolios, examination of lesson plans
Timeline: First semester of school year
Persons Responsible: Staff development committee, administrators, department chairs, master teachers
Budget: Funds necessary to purchase books and other professional development materials

References

Ausubel, D. P. (1968). *Educational psychology: A cognitive view*. New York: Holt, Rinehart and Winston.

Baddeley, A. D., & Hitch, G. J. (1994). Developments in the concept of working memory. *Neuropsychology, 8,* 485–493.

Bower, B. (1999, March 6). Learning may unify distant brain regions. *Science News* [On-line]. Available: www.findarticles.com.

Bowers, J. H., & Burkett, C. W. (1987). Relationship of student achievement and characteristics in two selected school facility environmental settings. (ERIC Document Reproduction Service No.: ED 286 278).

Brandt, R. (1999). Educators need to know about the human brain. *Phi Delta Kappan, 11,* 235–238.

Caine, G., & Caine, R. N. (2001). *The brain, education, and the competitive edge*. Lanham, MD: Scarecrow Education.

Campbell, D. (1997). *The Mozart effect: Tapping the power of music to heal the body, strengthen the mind, and unlock the creative spirit*. New York: Avon Books.

Claxton, C. S. (1990). Learning styles, minority students, and effective education. *Journal of Developmental Education, 14*(1), 6–8.

Cummings, J. L. (1995). Anatomic and behavioral aspects of frontal-subcortical circuits. *Annals of the New York Academy of Sciences, 769,* 1–13.

Dana, N. F. (1993). Elementary school preservice teachers' conceptions of social studies teaching and learning: A report on concept mapping. (ERIC Document Reproduction Service No.: ED 367 576).

Delpit, L. D. (1988). The silenced dialog: Power and pedagogy in educating other people's children. *Harvard Educational Review, 58,* 280–298.

D'Esposito, M., Detre, J. A., Alsop, D. C., Shin, R. K., Atlas, S., & Grossman, M. (1995). The neural basis of the central executive system of working memory. *Nature, 378,* 279–281.

Diamond, M., & Hopson, J. (1998). *Magic trees of the mind.* New York: Penguin.

Dixon, G., Poole, G. T., & Hamilton, S. (2000). The interrelationship of sociocultural, cognitive, and brain development: Classroom applications for African American and Hispanic children. *The NABSE, 4*(1), 26–34.

Fletcher, D. (1983). Effects of classroom lighting on the behavior of exceptional children. *Exceptional Education Quarterly, 4*(2), 75–89.

Gabriel, A. E. (1999). Brain-based learning: The scent of the trail. *Clearing House, 72,* 288–291.

Goleman, D. (1994). *Emotional intelligence.* New York: Bantam.

Goleman, D. (1998). *Working with emotional intelligence.* New York: Bantam.

Grangaard, E. M. (1995). Color and light effects on learning. (ERIC Document Reproduction Service No.: ED 382 381).

Greenfield, S. A. (1997). *The human brain: A guided tour.* New York: Basic Books.

Greenleaf, R. K. (1999). A neuroscience overview. Paper presented at the Learning & the Brain Conference, Washington, DC.

Hardiman, M. (2001). Connecting brain research with dimensions of learning. *Educational Leadership, 59*(3), 52–55.

Helmuth, L. (2001). Neuroscience: Dyslexia: Same brains, different languages. *Science.* Available: www.eLibrary.com.

Howard, P. J. (2000). *The owner's manual for the brain.* Atlanta: Bard Press.

Jensen, E. (2000). *Brain-based learning.* San Diego: The Brain Store.

Kalat, J. W. (2001). *Biological psychology.* Belmont, CA: Thomson Learning.

Kandel, E. R., & Squire, L. R. (2000). Neuroscience: Breaking down scientific barriers to the study of the brain and mind. *Science, 290,* 1113–1120.

Kosik, K. S., & Heschong, L. (2000). Daylight makes a difference: Daylight in the classroom can boost standardized test scores and learning. (ERIC Document Reproduction Service No.: ED 451 683).

Leamnson, R. (2000). Learning as biological brain change. *Change, 32*(6), 34–40.

LeDoux, J. (1996). *The emotional brain: The mysterious underpinnings of emotional life.* New York: Touchstone Books.

Lillard, P. P. (1972). *Montessori: A modern approach.* New York: Schocken Books.

Maryland State Department of Education. (2000). MSDE Content Standards. Available: www.MSDE.k12.md.us.

Marzano, R. J. (1992). *A different kind of classroom: Teaching with Dimensions of Learning.* Alexandria, VA: Association for Supervision and Curriculum Development.

Marzano, R. J., Pinkering, D. J., Arredondo, D. E., Blackburn, G. J., Brandt, R. S., & Moffett, C. A. (1992). *Dimensions of learning.* Alexandria, VA: Association for Supervision and Curriculum Development.

Marzano, R. J., Pinkering, D. J., & Pollock, J. E. (2001). *Classroom instruction that works.* Alexandria, VA: Association for Supervision and Curriculum Development.

McAleese, R., Garbinger, S., & Fisher, K. (1999). The knowledge arena: A learning environment that underpins concept mapping. (ERIC Document Reproduction Service No.: ED 429 970).

Nunley, K. F. (2002). How the adolescent brain challenges the adult brain. Available: http://help4teachers.com.

Ratey, J. J. (2001). *A user's guide to the brain.* New York: Vintage.

Restak, R. (1994). *The modular brain.* New York: Scribner.

Richards, T. L., Corina, D., Serafini, S., Steury, K., Echelard, D. R., Dager, S. R., Marro, K., Abbott, R. D., Maravilla, D. R., & Berninger, V. W. (2000). Effects of a phonologically driven treatment for dyslexia on lactate levels measured by proton MR spectroscopic imaging. *American Journal of Neuroradiology, 21,* 916–922.

Romo, R., Brody, C. D., Hernandez, A., & Lemus, L. (1999). Neuronal correlates of parametric working memory in the prefrontal cortex. *Nature, 397,* 520–522.

Sanders, M. G. (1997). Overcoming obstacles: Academic achievement as a response to racism and discrimination. *Journal of Negro Education, 66*(1), 83–93.

Schacter, D. (1996). *Searching for memory: The brain, the mind, and the past.* New York: Basic Books.

Semrud-Clikeman, M., Steingard, R. J., Filipeck, P., Biederman, J., Bekken, K., & Renshaw, P. F. (2000). Using MRI to examine brain-behavior relationships in males with attention deficit disorder with hyperactivity. *Journal of the American Academy of Child & Adolescent Psychiatry, 39*(4), 477–484.

Shaywitz, B. A., Pugh, K. R., Jenner, A. R., Fulbright, R. K., Fletcher, J. M., Gore, J. C., & Shaywitz, S. E. (2001). The neurobiology of reading and reading disability (dyslexia). In M. L. Kamil, P. B. Mosenthal, P. D. Pearson, & R. Barr (Eds.), *Handbook of reading* research (vol. 3, pp. 229–249). Mahwah, NJ: Lawrence Erlbaum Associates.

Sousa, D. A. (2001). *How the brain learns.* Thousand Oaks, CA: Corwin Press.

Sprenger, M. (1999). *Learning & memory.* Alexandria, VA: Association for Supervision and Curriculum Development.

Squire, L. R. (2002). Memory systems of the brain. *Learning brain expo: The brain store.* Available: www.thebrainstore.com.

Squire, L. R., & Kandel, E. R. (1999). *Memory: From mind to molecules.* New York: W. H. Freeman.

Stice, C. F., & Alvarez, M. C. (1986). Hierarchical concept mapping: Young children learning how to learn. (ERIC Document Reproduction Service No.: ED 274 946).

Sylwester, R. (1994). How emotions affect learning. *Educational Leadership, 52*(2), 28–32.

Turner, S. (2000). Study describes brain changes during learning. Providence, RI: Brown University News Service, October 19, 2000.

Wolff, P. (2001). *Brain matters.* Alexandria, VA: Association for Supervision and Curriculum Development.

Wolff, P., & Brandt, R. (1998). What do we know from brain research? *Educational Leadership, 56*(3), 8–13.

Zentall, S. S. (1983). Learning environments: A review of physical and temporal factors. *Exceptional Education Quarterly, 4*(2), 10–15.

Index

About the Author

In her career with the Baltimore city public school system, Mariale Hardiman has served as principal, assistant principal, department chair, and teacher. As staff developer and principal of Roland Park Elementary and Middle School since 1993, Ms. Hardiman has led the school to its designation as a Blue Ribbon School of Excellence. Under her leadership, the school has received numerous awards for continuous student achievement gains on both national standardized achievement tests and state performance assessments.

Ms. Hardiman also serves as adjunct instructor at Loyola College in Baltimore, Maryland. She earned her undergraduate and graduate degrees from Loyola College and her doctorate from Johns Hopkins University. Her article in the November 2001 issue of *Educational Leadership,* "Connecting Brain Research with Dimensions of Learning," has generated interest from educators worldwide. She is a frequent presenter at local, state, and national conferences and workshops.